Abhidhamma Studies

Abhidhamma Studies

Buddhist Explorations of Consciousness and Time

Nyanaponika Thera

Edited with an introduction by
Bhikkhu Bodhi

Wisdom Publications • Boston
in collaboration with the
Buddhist Publication Society
Kandy • Sri Lanka

WISDOM PUBLICATIONS
199 Elm Street
Somerville, Massachusetts 02144

First edition 1949 (Frewin & Co. Ltd., Colombo)
Second edition, revised and enlarged 1965 (BPS)
Third edition 1976, 1985 (BPS)
Fourth edition, revised and enlarged 1998 (Wisdom)

Library of Congress Cataloging-in-Publication Data

Nyanaponika, Thera, 1901-1994
Abhidhamma studies : Buddhist explorations of consciousness and time / Nyanaponika Thera ; edited with an introduction by Bhikkhu Bodhi.
p. cm.
Originally published: Colombo : Frewin, 1949.
Includes bibliographical references.
ISBN 0-86171-135-1 (alk. paper)
1. Abhidharma. 2. Tipiṭaka. Abhidhammapiṭaka. Dhammasaṅgaṇi––Criticism, interpretation, etc. I. Title.
BQ4195.N92 1998
294.3'824—dc21 97-38780

ISBN 0-86171-135-1

03 02 01 00 99
6 5 4 3 2

Design by: Adie Russell

Wisdom Publications' books are printed on acid-free paper and meet the guidelines for the permanence and durability of the Committee on Production Guidelines for Book Longevity of the Council on Library Resources.

Printed in the United States of America.

Contents

Publisher's Acknowledgment

The Publisher gratefully acknowledges the generous help of the Hershey Family Foundation in sponsoring the printing of this book.

Editor's Introduction

In his preface to this book Nyanaponika Thera explains that these studies originated while he was engaged in translating into German the *Dhammasaṅgaṇī* and the *Atthasālinī*, respectively the first book of the Pāli Abhidhamma Piṭaka and its authorized commentary. He translated these works during the trying years of World War II, while residing in the British civilian internment camp at Dehra Dun, in north India (1941–46). Unfortunately, these two translations, made with such keen understanding and appreciation of their subject, remain unpublished. The *Dhammasaṅgaṇī* appeared only in a very limited cyclostyle edition (Hamburg, 1950), long unavailable. The *Atthasālinī* has been in preparation for the press since the mid-1980s, but it is still uncertain whether it will ever see the light of day.

The investigations stimulated by this translation work, however, have enjoyed a happier fate. Soon after returning to Sri Lanka following the war, Ven. Nyanaponika recorded his reflections on the Abhidhamma in a set of four essays, which became the first version of this book, entitled *Abhidhamma Studies: Researches in Buddhist Psychology*. The manuscript must have been completed by 15 March 1947, the date of the preface, and was published in a series called Island Hermitage Publications (Frewin & Co. Ltd., Colombo, 1949). This imprint emanated from the Island Hermitage at Dodanduwa, a monastic settlement chiefly for Western Buddhist monks founded in 1911 by Ven. Nyanaponika's teacher, Ven. Nyanatiloka Mahāthera (1878–1957). Ven. Nyanatiloka, also from Germany, was the first Theravāda bhikkhu from continental Europe in modern times. Ordained in Burma in 1903, he soon established himself as an authority on the Abhidhamma, and it was from him that Ven. Nyanaponika acquired his deep respect for this abstruse branch of Buddhist learning.

While Island Hermitage Publications came to an early end, its animating spirit was reincarnated in the Buddhist Publication

Society (BPS), which Ven. Nyanaponika established in Kandy in 1958 together with two lay friends. Accordingly, in 1965 a second edition of *Abhidhamma Studies* appeared, published by the BPS. This edition had been stylistically polished (incorporating suggestions written into a copy of the first edition by Bhikkhu Ñāṇamoli) and included a new first chapter that served to explain the high esteem in which the Theravāda tradition holds the Abhidhamma. A third edition, issued in 1976, contained only minor corrections. For the present edition I have merely reformulated a few awkward sentences in the third edition, reorganized the notes, provided additional references, and supplied a bibliography. The subtitle has also been changed to convey a clearer idea of the book's contents.

Although these essays are largely intelligible on their own and can be read with profit even by those unacquainted with the Abhidhamma texts themselves, they will naturally be most rewarding if they are read with some awareness of the doctrinal and scriptural matrix from which they have emerged. While an introduction like this is certainly not the place for a thorough historical and doctrinal survey of the Abhidhamma, in what follows I will attempt to provide the reader with the information needed to place Ven. Nyanaponika's studies in their wider context. First I will briefly present an overview of the Abhidhamma literature on which he draws; then I will discuss the principal strains of Abhidhamma thought that underlie the essays; and finally, in the light of this background, I will highlight some of the ideas that Ven. Nyanaponika is attempting to convey in this book.

Before proceeding further I must emphasize at the outset that Ven. Nyanaponika's essays are not historical in orientation, and are thus very different in character from the well-known Abhidhamma studies of Erich Frauwallner, which attempt to trace the historical evolution of the Abhidhamma.[1] While he does make a few remarks on the historical authenticity of the Abhidhamma, for the most part he simply accepts the canonical Abhidhamma as a given point of departure and adopts toward this material an approach that is thoroughly philosophical and psychological. Though his focus is very narrow, namely, the first wholesome state of consciousness in the Consciousness chapter of the *Dhammasaṅgaṇī*, his treatment of this subject branches out into broader issues concerning the Abhidhamma analysis of mind and the bearings this has on the Buddhist spiritual life. The essays do not merely repeat the time-honored fundamentals of the Abhidhamma philosophy, but strike out in a direction that is innovative and boldly exploratory. Despite their strong rootedness in an ancient, minutely analytical corpus of knowledge, they venture into territory virtually untouched by the great Abhidhamma commentators of the past, raising questions and throwing out hypotheses with a depth of insight that is often exhilarating. It is this boldness of intuition, coupled with careful reflection and a capacity for mature judgment, that makes this little book a contemporary gem worthy of a place among the perennial classics of Abhidhamma literature.

The Abhidhamma Literature

The Abhidhamma is a comprehensive, systematic treatment of the Buddha's teachings that came to prominence in the Buddhist community during the first three centuries after the Master's death. The development of Abhidhamma spanned the broad spectrum of the early Buddhist schools, though the particular tracks that it followed in the course of its evolution differed markedly from one school to another. As each system of Abhidhamma assumed its individual contours, often in opposition to its rivals, the respective school responsible for it added a compilation of Abhidhamma treatises to its collection of authorized texts. In this way the original two canonical collections of the Buddha's Word—the Sutta and Vinaya Piṭakas—came to be augmented by a third collection, the Abhidhamma Piṭaka, thus giving us the familiar Tipiṭaka or "Three Baskets of the Doctrine."

There is some evidence, from the reports of the Chinese Buddhist pilgrims, that most of the old Indian Buddhist schools, if not all, had their own Abhidhamma Piṭakas. However, with the wholesale destruction of Buddhism in India in the twelfth century, all but three canonical Abhidhammas perished with hardly a trace.

The three exceptions are (1) the Theravāda version, in seven books, recorded in Pāli; (2) the Sarvāstivāda version, also in seven books but completely different from those of the Theravāda; and (3) a work called the *Śāriputra-abhidharma-śāstra*, probably belonging to the Dharmaguptaka school.[2] The Pāli Abhidhamma had survived because, long before Buddhism disappeared in India, it had been safely transplanted to Sri Lanka; the other two, because they had been brought to China and translated from Sanskrit into Chinese. Though the schools that nurtured these last two Abhidhamma systems vanished long ago, a late exposition of the Sarvāstivāda Abhidhamma system, Vasubandhu's *Abhidharmakośa*, continues to be studied among Tibetan Buddhists and in the Far East. In the Theravāda countries such as Sri Lanka, Myanmar, and Thailand, the Abhidhamma has always been a subject of vital interest, both among monks and educated lay Buddhists, and forms an essential component in any program of higher Buddhist studies. This is especially the case in Myanmar, which since the fifteenth century has been the heartland of Abhidhamma study in the Theravāda Buddhist world.

The seven treatises of the Pāli Abhidhamma Piṭaka are the *Dhammasaṅgaṇī*, the *Vibhaṅga*, the *Dhātukathā*, the *Puggalapaññatti*, the *Kathāvatthu*, the *Yamaka*, and the *Paṭṭhāna*. The distinctive features of the Abhidhamma methodology are not equally evident in all these works. In particular, the *Puggalapaññatti* is a detailed typology of persons that is heavily dependent on the Sutta Piṭaka, especially the Aṅguttara Nikāya; the *Kathāvatthu*, a polemical work offering a critical examination of doctrinal views that the Theravādin theorists considered deviations from the true version of the Dhamma. These two works do not exemplify the salient features of the Abhidhamma and may have been included in this Piṭaka merely as a matter of convenience. What is probably the most archaic core of Abhidhamma material—detailed definitions of the basic categories taken from the suttas, such as the aggregates, sense bases, and elements—is preserved in the *Vibhaṅga*. But the two works that best exemplify the mature version of the canonical Abhidhamma system are the *Dhammasaṅgaṇī* and the *Paṭṭhāna*. As Ven. Nyanaponika repeatedly points out, these two books are complementary and must be viewed together to obtain an adequate picture of the Abhidhamma methodology as a whole. The *Dhammasaṅgaṇī* emphasizes the analytical approach, its most notable achievement being the reduction of the complex panorama of experience to distinct mental and material phenomena, which are minutely defined and shown in their various combinations and classifications. The *Paṭṭhāna* advances a synthetic approach to the factors enumerated in the first book. It delineates the conditional relations that hold between the diverse mental and material phenomena disclosed by analysis, binding them together into a dynamic and tightly interwoven whole.

Each of the books of the Abhidhamma has its authorized commentary. Since the commentaries on the last five books are combined into one volume, there are three Abhidhamma commentaries: the *Atthasālinī* (on the *Dhammasaṅgaṇī*); the *Sammoha-vinodanī* (on the *Vibhaṅga*); and the *Pañcappakaraṇa-aṭṭhakathā* (on the other five books). These commentaries are the work of Ācariya Buddhaghosa, the most eminent of the Pāli commentators. Buddhaghosa was an Indian Buddhist monk who came to Sri Lanka in the fifth century C.E. to study the old Sinhalese commentaries (no longer extant) that had been preserved at the Mahāvihāra, the Great Monastery, the seat of Theravāda orthodoxy in Anuradhapura. On the basis of these old commentaries, written in a style of Sinhala that by then may have already been antiquated, he composed new commentaries in the internationally recognized Theravāda language, now known as Pāli. These commentaries, refined in expression and doctrinally coherent, are not original creative works expressing Buddhaghosa's own ideas, but edited and synoptic versions of the old commentaries, which had probably accumulated over several centuries and recorded the diverse opinions of the early generations of doctrinal specialists up to about the second century C.E. If we had direct access to these commentaries we would no doubt be able to trace the gradual evolution of the system of exegesis that finally became crystallized in the works of Buddhaghosa. Unfortunately, however, these old commentaries did not survive the ravages of time.

The Abhidhamma commentaries of Buddhaghosa do considerably more than explicate the difficult terms and statements of the canonical Abhidhamma texts. In the course of explication they introduce in full measure the reflections, discussions, judgments, and determinations of the ancient masters of the doctrine, which Buddhaghosa must have found in the old commentaries available to him. Thus, out of the beams and rafters of the canonical Abhidhamma, the commentaries construct a comprehensive and philosophically viable edifice that can be used for several purposes: the investigation of experience in the practice of insight meditation; the interpretation of the canonical Abhidhamma; and the interpretation of the other two Piṭakas, the Suttanta and the Vinaya, whose exegesis, at an advanced level, is guided by the principles of the Abhidhamma. Ācariya Buddhaghosa's masterpiece, the *Visuddhimagga*, is in effect a work of "applied Abhidhamma," and chapters 14–17 constitute a concise compendium of Abhidhamma theory as a preparation for insight meditation.

Following the age of the commentaries, Pāli Abhidhamma literature expanded by still another layer with the composition of the *ṭīkās*, the subcommentaries. Of these, the most important is the three-part *Mūlaṭīkā*, "The Fundamental (or Original) Subcommentary" to the three primary commentaries. This work is attributed to one Ācariya Ānanda, who may have worked in south India in the late fifth or early sixth century. Its purpose is to clarify obscure terms and ideas in the commentaries and also to shed additional light on the canonical texts. This work in turn has an *Anuṭīkā*, a secondary subcommentary, ascribed to Ācariya Dhammapāla, another south Indian.

Once the commentarial literature on the Abhidhamma had grown to gargantuan dimensions, the next stage in the development of Abhidhamma theory was governed by the need to reduce this material to more manageable proportions for easy use by teachers and their students. Thus there arrived the age of the Abhidhamma manuals, which reached its high point with the composition of the *Abhidhammattha-saṅgaha* sometime between the tenth and twelfth centuries. This work, ascribed to one Ācariya Anuruddha, occupies only fifty pages in print, yet provides a masterly overview of the whole Abhidhamma, both canonical and commentarial, in an easily memorizable form. The *Saṅgaha* has become the standard primer for Abhidhamma studies throughout the Theravāda Buddhist world, and in the traditional system of education teachers require their pupils to learn it by heart as the prerequisite for further lessons in the Abhidhamma. Yet, because the manual is so terse and pithy in expression, when read on its own it borders on the cryptic, and to convey any clear meaning it needs paraphrase and explanation. Thus the *Saṅgaha* in its turn has generated a massive commentarial literature, written both in Sri Lanka and Myanmar, and this has opened up still new avenues for the elaboration of Abhidhamma theory. In this way the literary history of the Abhidhamma has advanced by a rhythmic alternation of condensed and expansive modes of treatment, the systole and diastole phases in the evolution of Theravāda Buddhist doctrine.

From this quick and superficial overview of the Abhidhamma literature we can see that the fountainhead of the Pāli Abhidhamma system is the Abhidhamma Piṭaka with its seven treatises. But how did this collection of texts come into being? To this question, the Theravāda commentarial tradition and present-day critical scholarship give different answers. Unlike the suttas and the accounts of the monastic rules in the Vinaya, the books of the canonical Abhidhamma do not provide any information about their own origins. The commentaries, however, ascribe these treatises to the Buddha himself. The *Atthasālinī*, which gives the most explicit account, states that the Buddha realized the Abhidhamma at the foot of the Bodhi Tree on the night of his enlightenment and investigated it in detail during the fourth week after the enlightenment, while sitting in deep meditation in a house of gems (*ratanaghara*) to the northeast of the Bodhi Tree. Subsequently, during his career as a teacher, he spent one rains retreat in the Tāvatiṁsa heaven, where he taught the Abhidhamma to the devas or gods from ten thousand world systems. Each morning during this period he would descend to the human realm for his one meal of the day, and then he taught the methods or principles (*naya*) of the doctrine that he had covered to his chief disciple Sāriputta, who elaborated them for the benefit of his own pupils.[3]

Although this account still prevails in conservative monastic circles in the Theravāda world, critical scholarship has been able to determine in broad outline, by comparative study of the various Abhidhamma texts available, the route along which the canonical Abhidhamma evolved. These studies indicate that before it came to constitute a clearly articulated system the Abhidhamma had gradually taken shape over several centuries. The word *abhidhamma* itself appears already in the suttas, but in contexts that indicate that it was a subject discussed by the monks themselves rather than a type of teaching given to them by the Buddha.[4] Sometimes the word *abhidhamma* is paired with *abhivinaya*, and we might suppose that the two terms respectively refer to a specialized, analytical treatment of the doctrine and the monastic discipline. Several suttas suggest that these Abhidhamma discussions proceeded by posing questions and offering replies. If we are correct in assuming that these ancient discussions were one of the seeds of the codified Abhidhamma, then their catechistic framework would explain the prominence of the "interrogation sections" (*pañhāvāra*) in the canonical Abhidhamma treatises.

Another factor that contemporary scholarship regards as a seed for the development of the Abhidhamma was the use of certain master lists to represent the conceptual structure of the Buddha's teachings. For the sake of easy memorization and as an aid to exposition, the doctrinal specialists in the early Sangha often cast the teachings into outline form. These outlines, which drew upon the numerical sets that the Buddha himself regularly used as the scaffolding for his doctrine, were not mutually exclusive but overlapped and meshed in ways that allowed them to be integrated into master lists that resembled a tree diagram. Such master lists were called *mātikās*, "matrixes," and skill in their use was sometimes included among the qualifications of an erudite monk.[5] To be skilled in the *mātikās* it was necessary to know not only the terms and their definitions but also their underlying structures and architectonic arrangement, which revealed the inner logic of the Dhamma. An early phase of Abhidhamma activity must have consisted in the elaboration of these master lists, a task that would have required extensive knowledge of the teachings and a capacity for rigorous, technically precise thought. The existing Abhidhamma Piṭakas include substantial sections devoted to such elaborations, and beneath them we can hear the echoes of the early discussions in the Sangha that culminated in the first Abhidhamma texts.

While the roots from which the Abhidhamma sprang can be traced back to the early Sangha, perhaps even during the Buddha's lifetime, the different systems clearly assumed their mature expression only after the Buddhist community had split up into distinct schools with their own doctrinal peculiarities. Codified and authorized Abhidhamma texts must have been in circulation by the third century B.C., the time of the Third (exclusively Theravādin) Council, which was held in Pāṭaliputta, the capital of King Aśoka's Mauryan empire. These texts, which would have constituted the original nuclei of the Theravāda and Sarvāstivāda Abhidhamma Piṭakas, might have continued to evolve for several more centuries. In the first century B.C. the Theravāda Abhidhamma Piṭaka, along with the rest of the Pāli Canon, was formally written down for the first time, at the Ālokavihāra in Sri Lanka. This officially approved recension of the Abhidhamma Piṭaka must mark the terminal point of its development in the Pāli school, though it is conceivable that minor additions were incorporated even afterward.

The Abhidhamma Teaching

The Abhidhamma teaching in the *Dhammasaṅgaṇī*, the focus of Ven. Nyanaponika's essays, might be discussed in terms of three interwoven strands of thought: (1) an underlying ontology framed in terms of bare ontological factors called *dhammas*; (2) the use of an "attribute-*mātikā*," a methodical list of contrasting qualities, as a grid for classifying the factors resulting from ontological analysis; and (3) the elaboration of a detailed typology of consciousness as a way of mapping the *dhammas* in relation to the ultimate goal of the Dhamma, the attainment of Nibbāna. The first two strands are shared by the Theravāda and Sarvāstivāda systems (though with differences in the details) and might be seen as stemming from the original archaic core of Abhidhamma analysis. The third strand, the minute analysis of consciousness, seems to be a specific feature of the Pāli Abhidhamma and thus may have evolved only after the two traditions had gone their separate ways.

We will now discuss these three strands of Abhidhamma thought more fully.

1. *The Dhamma Theory.* Although Ven. Nyanaponika distinguishes between phenomenology and ontology and assigns the Abhidhamma to the former rather than the latter, he does so on the assumption that ontology involves the quest for "an essence, or ultimate principle, underlying the phenomenal world" (p. 19). If, however, we understand ontology in a wider sense as the philosophical discipline concerned with determining what really exists, with discriminating between the real and the apparent, then we could justly claim that the Abhidhamma is built upon an ontological vision. This vision has been called the *dhamma* theory.[6] The theory as such is not articulated in the Abhidhamma Piṭaka, which rarely makes explicit the premises that underlie its systematizing projects, but comes into prominence only in the later commentarial literature, particularly in the commentaries to the Abhidhamma manuals. Succinctly stated, this theory maintains that the manifold of phenomenal existence is made up of a multiplicity of "thing-events" called *dhammas*, which are the realities that conceptual thought works upon to fabricate the consensual world of everyday reality. But the *dhammas*, though constitutive of experience, are distinctly different from the gross entities resulting from the operations of conceptual thought. Unlike the persisting persons and objects of everyday reality, the *dhammas* are evanescent occurrences, momentary mental and physical happenings brought into being through conditions—with the sole exception of the unconditioned element, Nibbāna, which is the one *dhamma* that is not evanescent or subject to conditions.

The germ of the *dhamma* theory can already be found in the suttas, in the Buddha's instructions aimed at the development of wisdom (*paññā*). For wisdom or insight to arise, the meditator must learn to suspend the normal constructive, synthesizing activity of the mind responsible for weaving the reams of immediate sensory data into coherent narrative patterns revolving around persons, entities, and their attributes. Instead, the meditator must adopt a radically phenomenological stance, attending mindfully to each successive occasion of experience exactly as it presents itself in its sheer immediacy. When this technique of "bare attention" is assiduously applied, the familiar world of everyday perception dissolves into a dynamic stream of impersonal phenomena, flashes of actuality arising and perishing with incredible rapidity. It is the thing-events discerned in the stream of immediate experience, the constitutive mental and physical phenomena, that are called *dhammas*, and it is with their characteristics, modes of occurrence, classifications, and relationships that the Abhidhamma is primarily concerned.

To assist the meditator in applying this phenomenological investigation of experience, the Buddha had delineated various conceptual schemes that group these bare phenomena into orderly sets. These sets are governed by different heuristic principles, of which we might distinguish three: the disclosure of the phenomenal field; the causes of bondage and suffering; and the aids to enlightenment.

The *disclosure of the phenomenal field* aims at showing how all the factors of existence function in unison without a substantial self behind them to serve as a permanent subject or directing agent. The conceptual schemes used for this purpose include the five aggregates (*pañcakkhandhā*: material form, feeling, perception, mental formations, and consciousness); the six internal and external sense bases (*saḷāyatana*: the six sense faculties including mind and their respective objects); and the eighteen elements (*aṭṭhārasa dhātuyo*: the six senses, their objects, and the corresponding types of consciousness).

The *causes of bondage and suffering* are the defilements, the main impediments to spiritual progress, which include such groups as the four taints (*āsava*), the four kinds of clinging (*upādāna*), the five hindrances (*nīvaraṇa*), and the ten fetters (*saṁyojana*).

The *aids to enlightenment* are the various sets of training factors that make up the Buddhist path to liberation. These are traditionally grouped into seven sets with a total of thirty-seven factors: the four foundations of mindfulness, the four right efforts, the four bases of accomplishment, the five spiritual faculties, the five powers, the seven factors of enlightenment, and the eight factors of the Noble Eightfold Path.

One of the major projects that the Abhidhamma Piṭaka sets for itself is to collect these various schemes into a systematic whole in which each item has a clearly defined position. To fulfill this aim, the architects of the Abhidhamma did not simply pile up lists but attempted to coordinate them, establish correspondences, and display relationships. Through their research into the *dhammas*, the Abhidhamma masters discovered that diverse terms used by the Buddha for the pedagogical purposes of his teaching often represent, at the level of actuality, the same factor functioning in different ways or under different aspects. Thus, for example, "clinging to sensual pleasures" among the four kinds of clinging is identical with the hindrance of sensual desire among the five hindrances; the practice of mindfulness in the four foundations of mindfulness is identical with the faculty of mindfulness among the five faculties and also with the path factor of right mindfulness in the Eightfold Path; the sense base of mind among the six senses is identical with the aggregate of consciousness among the five aggregates, and both comprise the seven consciousness elements among the eighteen elements.

By proceeding thus, the Abhidhamma draws up a fixed list of ontological actualities that it understands to be the differently colored threads that constitute the inconceivably diverse and complex fabric of experience. These ontological actualities are the *dhammas*, which the later Pāli Abhidhamma neatly groups into four classes of ultimates (*paramattha-dhamma*) comprising eighty-two actualities: consciousness (*citta*), which is one reality with eighty-nine or 121 types; fifty-two mental factors (*cetasika*); twenty-eight kinds of material phenomena (*rūpa*); and one unconditioned element, Nibbāna. The various defilements and aids to enlightenment are traced to particular mental factors (with the exception of one "base of accomplishment," the *citta-iddhipāda*, which is consciousness itself), and a detailed scheme is drawn up to show how the mental factors combine in the acts of consciousness and how the mental side of experience is correlated with the material world.

2. *The Attribute-mātikā.* Having reduced the entire manifold of

experience to a procession of impersonal thing-events, the Abhidhamma sets about to classify them according to a scheme determined by the guiding ideals of the Dhamma. This scheme is embedded in a *mātikā* or master list of contrasting categories. But since the lists of *dhammas* resulting from ontological analysis can also be called *mātikās*, following Frauwallner we might refer to the master list of qualitative categories as an attribute-*mātikā*.

The attribute-*mātikā* is announced at the very beginning of the *Dhammasaṅgaṇī* and serves as a preface to the entire Abhidhamma Piṭaka. It consists of 122 modes of classification proper to the Abhidhamma system, with an additional forty-two taken from the suttas. Of the Abhidhamma modes, twenty-two are triads (*tika*), sets of three terms used to classify the fundamental factors of existence; the other hundred are dyads (*duka*), binary terms used as a basis for categorization. The triads include such sets as states that are wholesome, unwholesome, indeterminate; states associated with pleasant feeling, with painful feeling, with neutral feeling; states that are kamma results, states productive of kamma results, states that are neither; and so forth. The dyads include roots, not roots; having roots, not having roots; conditioned states, unconditioned states; mundane states, supramundane states; and so forth. Within these dyads we also find the various defilements: taints, fetters, knots, floods, bonds, hindrances, misapprehensions, clingings, corruptions. The *mātikā* also includes forty-two dyads taken from the suttas, but these have a different character from the Abhidhamma sets and do not figure elsewhere in the system.

The *Dhammasaṅgaṇī* devotes two full chapters to the definition of the *mātikā*, which is done by specifying which *dhammas* are endowed with the attributes included in each triad and dyad. In chapter 3 this is done by way of the classical scheme of categories, such as the five aggregates, and in chapter 4 again by means of a simpler, more concise method of explanation. The same *mātikā* also figures prominently in the *Vibhaṅga* and the *Dhātukathā*, while in the *Paṭṭhāna* it is integrated with the system of conditional relations to generate a vast work of gigantic proportions that enumerates all the conceivable relations between all the items included under the Abhidhamma triads and dyads.

3. *The Typology of Consciousness.* To fill out our picture of the project undertaken in the *Dhammasaṅgaṇī,* and more widely in the Abhidhamma as a whole, we need to bring in another element, in some respects the most important. This is the medium within which the Abhidhamma locates its systematic treatment of experience, namely, consciousness or mind (*citta*). The Abhidhamma is above all an investigation of the possibilities of the mind, and thus its most impressive achievement is the construction of an elaborate map revealing the entire topography of consciousness. Like all maps, the one devised by the Abhidhamma necessarily simplifies the terrain which it depicts, but again like any well-planned map its simplification is intended to serve a practical purpose. In this case the map is drawn up to guide the seeker through the tangle of mental states discerned in meditative experience toward the aim of the Buddha's teaching, liberation from suffering. For this reason the map devised by the Abhidhamma looks very different from a map of the mind that might be drawn up by a Western psychologist as an aid to understanding psychological disorders. The Buddhist map makes no mention of neuroses, complexes, or fixations. Its two poles are bondage and liberation, saṁsāra and Nibbāna, and the specific features it represents are those states of mind that prolong our bondage and misery in saṁsāra, those that are capable of leading to mundane happiness and higher rebirths, and those that lead out from the whole cycle of rebirths to final deliverance in Nibbāna.

In delineating its typology of consciousness the Abhidhamma extends to both the microscopic and macroscopic levels the concern with the functioning of mind already so evident in the Sutta Piṭaka. In the suttas the Buddha declares that mind is the forerunner of all things and the chief determinant of human destiny, and he holds up the challenge of self-knowledge and mental self-mastery as the heart of his liberative discipline. In the suttas, however, concern with theoretical investigation is subordinated to the pragmatic aims of the training, and thus the analysis and description of mental states remains fairly simple. In the *Dhammasaṅgaṇī,* where theoretical concerns are given free rein, the analysis and classification of consciousness is pursued relentlessly in a quest for systematic completeness.

The schematization of consciousness is undertaken as a way of fleshing out the first triad of the *mātikā*, and thus the primary distinctions drawn between mental states are framed in terms of ethical quality: into the wholesome, the unwholesome, and the indeterminate. The *Dhammasaṅgaṇī* shows that the entire domain of consciousness in all its diversity is bound into an orderly cosmos by two overarching laws: first, the mundane moral law of kamma and its fruit, which links mundane wholesome and unwholesome states of consciousness to their respective results, the fruits of kamma, the latter included in the class of indeterminate consciousness. The second is the liberative or transcendent law by which certain wholesome states of consciousness—the supramundane paths—produce their own results, the four fruits of liberation, culminating in the attainment of Nibbāna.

The *Dhammasaṅgaṇī* first takes up wholesome consciousness (*kusala-citta*) and distinguishes it into four planes: (1) sense sphere, (2) form sphere (i.e., the consciousness of the four or five mundane jhānas), (3) formless sphere (i.e., the consciousness of the four formless meditations), and (4) supramundane (i.e., the consciousness of the four noble paths, which become twentyfold when correlated with the five supramundane jhānas). Second, unwholesome consciousness (*akusala-citta*) is analyzed into twelve types, as determined by the unwholesome roots from which they spring, that is, as rooted in greed, or in hatred, or in bare delusion. Third, kammically indeterminate consciousness (*abyākata-citta*) is considered, states of mind that are neither wholesome nor unwholesome. This is first bifurcated into resultant consciousness (*vipāka-citta*) and functional consciousness (*kiriya-citta*), which in turn are each used as headings for classifying their subordinate types. In this way the *Dhammasaṅgaṇī* builds up a typology of 121 acts of consciousness (*citt'uppāda*), each of which is a complex whole made up of consciousness itself, *citta*, the bare knowing of an object, functioning in correlation with various mental constituents, the *cetasikas*, which perform more specific tasks in the act of cognition.

The analysis of each type of consciousness proceeds by asking what states are present on an occasion when such a state of consciousness has arisen, and this provides the opportunity for minutely dissecting that state of consciousness into its components. The constituents of the conscious occasion are enumerated, not in the abstract (as is done in the later Abhidhamma manuals) but as members of fixed sets generally selected from the suttas. The first set consists of five bare cognitive elements present on any occasion of cognition: sense-contact, feeling, perception, volition, and consciousness. Following this, various other sets are introduced, and their components are defined by fixed formulas.

The following chapter of the *Dhammasaṅgaṇī* undertakes, in a similar way, a detailed analysis of material phenomena, which are all comprised under the heading of states that are kammically indeterminate (*abyākata*: neither wholesome nor unwholesome). Since Ven. Nyanaponika barely touches on the Abhidhamma treatment of material phenomena, we need not pursue this discussion further.

The Present Book

Chronologically and structurally, the essays that make up *Abhidhamma Studies* unfold from chapters 3 and 4, which deal with the first type of wholesome consciousness analyzed in the *Dhammasaṅgaṇī*. Although this section forms only a fraction of the treatise, it offers the key to the entire first chapter, the Analysis of Consciousness, and thus an investigation of its terms and methodology has major significance for an understanding of the Abhidhamma system as a whole. Chapter 3 presents the Pāli text and an English translation of the opening paragraph on the first type of wholesome consciousness; Chapter 4, a detailed investigation of its meaning and implications. Chapter 5 reverts to the opening formula for the first state of wholesome consciousness, which establishes time as an essential dimension of conscious experience. Taking up a verse in the *Atthasālinī* as his point of departure, Ven. Nyanaponika explores a number of signposts that the Abhidhamma holds out for understanding the relationship between time and consciousness.

Chapter 2 was added to balance the emphasis on analysis that predominates in the last three chapters of the book. Under the title

"The Twofold Method of Abhidhamma Philosophy" Ven. Nyanaponika cautions us that a complete perspective on the Abhidhamma requires us to take account, not only of the analytical treatment of experience so conspicuous in the first three Abhidhamma treatises, but also of the synthetical approach that predominates in the last treatise, the *Paṭṭhāna*, wherein all the terms resulting from analysis are connected to one another by a vast network of conditional relations. Chapter 1 was written last, and was added to the book only in the second edition. Its purpose is to defend the Abhidhamma against common criticisms, both ancient and modern, and to establish its legitimacy as an authentic Buddhist enterprise that can make important contributions to Buddhist theory and practice.

Viewed in its wider context, *Abhidhamma Studies* is both an emphatic affirmation of the high value that Buddhist tradition ascribes to the Abhidhamma and a trenchant attempt to break through the shackles that have tended to stultify traditional Abhidhamma study. Ven. Nyanaponika already sounds this radical note in his preface, when he declares that the Abhidhamma is "meant for inquiring and searching spirits who are not satisfied by monotonously and uncritically repeating ready-made terms." Reading behind these lines we can obtain some picture of what Abhidhamma study has too often become in Theravādin scholastic circles: an exercise in blindly absorbing by rote a hallowed body of knowledge and passing it on to others with only scant concern for its deeper relevance to the spiritual life. For Ven. Nyanaponika, the Abhidhamma, like Buddhism as a whole, is a living dynamic organism, and his underlying purpose in this book is to breathe new life into this sometimes moribund creature.

Throughout his essays Ven. Nyanaponika repeatedly cautions us against another, closely related tendency in traditional Abhidhamma studies: that of allowing Abhidhamma learning to degenerate into a dry and barren intellectual exercise. He holds that the study of Abhidhamma and the practice of meditation must proceed hand in hand. The study of Abhidhamma, at least by way of its fundamental principles, helps to correct misinterpretations of meditative experience and also, in relation to insight meditation, lays bare the phenomena that must be discerned and comprehended in the course of contemplation. Meditation, in turn, brings the Abhidhamma to life and translates its abstract conceptual schemes into living experience. The Abhidhamma itself, he holds, has immense significance for a correct understanding of the Dhamma, for it spells out, with striking thoroughness and precision, the two mutually reinforcing intuitions that lie at the very heart of the Buddha's enlightenment: the principle of *anattā* or non-self, and the principle of *paṭicca-samuppāda*, the dependent origination of all phenomena of existence.

If I had to single out one strain in Ven. Nyanaponika's thought as his major contribution to our understanding of the Abhidhamma philosophy, I would choose his emphasis on the inherent dynamism of the original Theravāda version of the Abhidhamma. It is especially necessary to stress this point because the treatment of the Abhidhamma that has come down to us in the medieval manuals can convey the impression that the Abhidhamma is a rigid, static, even myopic system that would reduce the profound, mind-transforming Dhamma of enlightenment to a portfolio of orderly charts. For Ven. Nyanaponika, the ancient canonical Abhidhamma is as vital and dynamic as the reality it is intended to depict, vibrant with intuitions that cannot easily be captured in numerical lists and tables. The key he offers us for restoring to this system its original dynamism is a recognition of the essentially temporal dimension of experience. Temporality is intrinsic to the description of conscious states throughout the *Dhammasaṅgaṇī*, but it is easy to overlook its importance when the subtle complexities of the system are subordinated to a concern for schematic representation, as occurs in the later literature. For Ven. Nyanaponika it is only by attending to the time factor that we can rediscover, in the Abhidhamma, the depth and breadth of primary experience and the dignity and decisive potency of the present moment.[7]

To recover this element of dynamic temporality, Ven. Nyanaponika points us away from the systematic manuals of the medieval period back toward the canonical texts themselves, the Abhidhamma Piṭaka. This does not mean that he slights the manuals or disparages their contribution. He recognizes that these works serve a valuable purpose by compressing and organizing into a compact, digestible format a vast mass of material that might otherwise intimidate and overwhelm a novice student of the subject. What he maintains, however, is that familiarity with the manuals is not sufficient. Illuminating and fruitful lines of thought lie hidden in the original texts, and it is only by unearthing these through deep inquiry and careful reflection that the riches of the Abhidhamma can be extracted and made available, not to Buddhist studies alone but to all contemporary attempts to understand the nature of human experience.

It had always been one of Nyanaponika Thera's deepest wishes to resume the methodical exploration of the Abhidhamma, which he had broken off after completing the essays contained in the present volume. His life's circumstances and own inner needs, however, did not permit this. During the early 1950s an increased concern with his own spiritual development led him to pursue more vigorously the practice of meditation, which bore fruit in his popular book *The Heart of Buddhist Meditation.* In the mid-1950s he had to attend on his ailing teacher, Ven. Nyanatiloka Mahāthera, and to meet certain commitments regarding literary work in German, which included the revision and editing of his teacher's German translation of the complete Aṅguttara Nikāya. Then in 1958 the Buddhist Publication Society was born, which he conscientiously served as president and editor of until his retirement in the 1980s, by which time his sight had deteriorated too far to allow any further literary work.

Nevertheless, in this small volume Ven. Nyanaponika has left us one of the most original, profound, and stimulating contributions in English toward the understanding of this ancient yet so contemporary system of philosophical psychology. It is to be hoped that these studies will in some way serve to fulfill the hope the author expressed in his preface, that they will "show modern independent thinkers new vistas and open new avenues of thought," thereby vindicating the eternal and fundamental truths made known by the Buddha.

Bhikkhu Bodhi

Preface

These studies originated when the author was engaged in translating into German the *Dhammasaṅgaṇī* ("Compendium of Phenomena") and its commentary, the *Atthasālinī*. These two books are the starting point and the main subject of the following pages that, in part, may serve as a kind of fragmentary subcommentary to them.

The content of these studies is rather varied: they include philosophical and psychological investigations, references to the practical application of the teachings concerned, pointers to neglected or unnoticed aspects of the Abhidhamma, textual research, etc. This variety of contents serves to show that wherever we dig deep enough into that inexhaustible mine, the Abhidhamma literature, we shall meet with valuable contributions to the theoretical understanding and practical realization of Buddhist doctrine. So the main purpose of these pages is to stimulate further research in the field of Abhidhamma to a much wider and deeper extent than was possible in this modest attempt.

There is no reason why the Abhidhamma philosophy of the Southern or Theravāda tradition should stagnate today or why its further development should not be resumed. In fact, through many centuries there has been a living growth of Abhidhamma thought, and even in our own days there are original contributions to it from Burma, for example, by that remarkable monk-philosopher, the Venerable Ledi Sayadaw. There are a vast number of subjects in the canonical and commentarial Abhidhamma literature that deserve and require closer investigation and new presentation in the language of our time. There are many lines of thought, only briefly sketched in Abhidhamma tradition, that merit detailed treatment in connection with parallel tendencies in modern thought. Finally, in some important subjects of Abhidhamma doctrine we must deplore the partial loss of ancient tradition, a fact that is clearly indicated by the appearance of technical terms nowhere explained.

Here a careful and conscientious restoration in conformity with the spirit of the Theravāda tradition is required unless we would relegate those parts of the Abhidhamma to the status of venerable but fragmentary museum pieces.

Abhidhamma is meant for inquiring and searching spirits who are not satisfied by monotonously and uncritically repeating ready-made terms, even if these are Abhidhamma terms. Abhidhamma is for imaginative minds who are able to fill in, as it were, the columns of the tabulations, for which the canonical Abhidhamma books have furnished the concise headings. The Abhidhamma is not for those timid souls who are not content that a philosophical thought should not actually contradict Buddhist tradition, but demand that it must be expressly, even literally, supported by canonical or commentarial authority. Such an attitude is contrary to the letter and the spirit of the Buddha-Dhamma. It would mean that the Abhidhamma philosophy must remain within the limits of whatever has been preserved of the traditional exegetical literature and hence will cease to be a living and growing organism. This would certainly be deplorable for many reasons.

We are convinced that the Abhidhamma, if suitably presented, could also enrich modern non-Buddhist thought, in philosophy as well as psychology. To state parallels with modern Western thought or the historical precedence of Buddhist versions is not so important in itself. It is more important that the Buddhist way of presenting and solving the respective problems should show modern independent thinkers new vistas and open new avenues of thought, which in turn might revive Buddhist philosophy in the East. We are convinced that from such a philosophical exchange there would arise a glorious vindication of those eternal and fundamental truths, at once simple and profound, that the greatest genius of humankind, the Buddha, proclaimed.

Nyanaponika Thera

I

The Abhidhamma Philosophy

Its Estimation in the Past, Its Value for the Present

THE HIGH ESTEEM FOR ABHIDHAMMA IN BUDDHIST TRADITION

The Abhidhamma Piṭaka, or the Philosophical Collection, forms the third great section of the Buddhist Pāli Canon (Tipiṭaka). In its most characteristic parts it is a system of classifications, analytical enumerations, and definitions, with no discursive treatment of the subject matter. In particular its two most important books, the *Dhammasaṅgaṇī* and the *Paṭṭhāna,* have the appearance of huge collections of systematically arranged tabulations, accompanied by definitions of the terms used in the tables. This, one would expect, is a type of literature scarcely likely to gain much popular appreciation. Yet the fact remains that the Abhidhamma has always been highly esteemed and even venerated in the countries of Theravāda Buddhism.

Two examples taken from the chronicles of Sri Lanka illustrate this high regard for the Abhidhamma. In the tenth century C.E., on the order of King Kassapa V, the whole Abhidhamma Piṭaka was inscribed on gold plates, and the first of these books, the *Dhammasaṅgaṇī,* was set with jewels. When the work was completed, the precious manuscripts were taken in a huge procession to a beautiful monastery and deposited there. Another king of Lanka, Vijayabāhu (eleventh century), used to study the *Dhammasaṅgaṇī* in the early morning before he took up his royal duties, and he prepared a translation of it into Sinhala, which however has not been preserved.

What were the reasons for such an extraordinary esteem for

material that appears at first glance to consist of no more than dry and unattractive textbooks? And what actual importance do the two basic works of the Abhidhamma in particular, the *Dhammasaṅgaṇī* and the *Paṭṭhāna,* still have today? These are the questions that we shall attempt to answer here.

In considering the reasons for this high esteem and regard for the Abhidhamma, we may leave aside any manifestation of faith, more or less unquestioning, that evokes in the devotee a certain awe owing to the very abstruseness and bulk of these books. That apart, we may find a first explanation in the immediate impression on susceptible minds that they are faced here by a gigantic edifice of penetrative insight, which in its foundations and its layout cannot well be ascribed to a lesser mind than that of a Buddha; and this first impression will find growing confirmation in the gradual process of comprehending these teachings.

According to the Theravāda tradition the Abhidhamma is the domain proper of the Buddhas (*buddhavisaya*), and its initial conception in the Master's mind (*manasā desanā*) is traced to the time immediately after the Great Enlightenment. It was in the fourth of the seven weeks spent by the Master in the vicinity of the Bodhi Tree that the Abhidhamma was conceived.[8] These seven days were called by the teachers of old "the Week of the House of Gems" (*ratanaghara-sattāha*). "The House of Gems" is indeed a very befitting expression for the crystal-clear edifice of Abhidhamma thought in which the Buddha dwelt during that period.

The Abhidhamma as System and Method

Those who have an eye for the ingenious and the significant in the architecture of great edifices of thought will probably be impressed first by the Abhidhamma's structural qualities, its wide compass, its inner consistency, and its far-reaching implications. The Abhidhamma offers an impressive systematization of the whole of reality as far as it is of concern to the final goal of the Buddha's teaching—liberation from craving and suffering; for it deals with actuality from an exclusively ethical and psychological viewpoint and with a definite practical purpose.

A strikingly impressive feature of the Abhidhamma is its analysis of the entire realm of consciousness. The Abhidhamma is the first historical attempt to map the possibilities of the human mind in a thorough and realistic way, without admixture of metaphysics and mythology. This system provides a method by which the enormous welter of facts included or implied in it can be subordinated to, and be utilized by, the *liberating* function of knowledge, which in the Buddha's teaching is the essential task and the greatest value of true understanding. This organizing and mustering of knowledge for such a purpose cannot fail to appeal to the practical thinker.

The Abhidhamma may also be regarded as a systematization of the doctrines contained, or implicit, in the Sutta Piṭaka, the Collection of Discourses. It formulates these doctrines in strictly philosophical (*paramattha*) or truly realistic (*yathābhūta*) language that as far as possible employs terms descriptive of functions and processes without any of the conventional (*vohāra*) and unrealistic concepts that assume a personality, an agent (as different from the act), a soul, or a substance.

These remarks about the systematizing import of the Abhidhamma may perhaps create the impression in the reader that the Abhidhamma is no more than "a mere method with only a formalistic function." Leaving aside the fact that this is not so, as we shall see later, let us first quote, against this somewhat belittling attitude, a word of Friedrich Nietzsche, himself certainly no friend of rigid systematization: "Scientific spirit rests upon insight into the method."

For the preeminently practical needs of the Buddhist the Abhidhamma fulfills the requirements stated by Bertrand Russell: "A complete description of the existing world would require not only a catalogue of the things, but also a mention of all their qualities and relations."[9] A systematic "catalogue of things" together with their qualities, or better "functions," is given in the first book of the Abhidhamma, the *Dhammasaṅgaṇī*, a title that could well be rendered "A Catalogue (or Compendium) of Things"; and the relations, or the conditionality, of these things are treated in the *Paṭṭhāna*.

Some who consider themselves "strong-minded" have called systems "a refuge of feeble minds." While it must be admitted that the conceptual labels supplied by systems (including the Abhidhamma) have often been misused as a surrogate for correct comprehension of reality, this does not mean that the fault lies in systematic thought itself. The fault lies, rather, in the attitude with which a system is developed and the use to which it is put. If systematic thought is cautiously and critically applied, it can fulfill a valuable function, providing "weapons of defense" against the overwhelming assault of innumerable internal and external impressions on the human mind. This unceasing influx of impressions, by sheer weight of number and diversity alone, can be either overpowering and fascinating or else confusing, intimidating, distracting, even dissolving. The only means by which the human mind can assimilate this vast world of plurality (*papañca*), at least partly, is with the aid of systematic and methodical thought. But systems may also be "aggressive weapons" when wielded by a mind that through its power of understanding tries to control and master the numerous experiences, actions, and reactions occurring in our inner and outer world, subordinating them to its own purposes.

The Abhidhamma system, however, is not concerned with an artificial, abstract world of "objects in themselves." Insofar as it deals with external facts at all, the respective concepts relate those "external facts" to the bondage or liberation of the human mind; or they are terms auxiliary to the tasks of the understanding and mental training connected with the work of liberation.

The basically dynamic character of the Abhidhamma system, and of the concepts it employs, goes far in preventing both rigidity and any artificial simplification of a complex and ever-changing world—the faults that those inimical to them find in all "systems."

System and method bring order, coherence, and meaning into what often appears to be a world of isolated facts, which becomes amenable to our purposes only by a methodical approach. This holds true for the system of the Abhidhamma, too, in regard to the highest purpose: mind's liberation from ignorance and suffering.

Clarification of Terms

Many thinkers of all times and cultures have insisted that a clarification of concepts and terms is a necessary basis for realistic and effective thought and action; indeed, Confucius says it is even a condition for proper governance. But throughout history the widespread confusion of ideas that has steered human destiny shows that such conceptual clarification has been neglected in nearly all branches of life and thought—a fact responsible for much misery and destruction.

It is another evidence of the scientific spirit of the Abhidhamma that the definition of its terms and of their range of application occupies a very prominent place. In particular, the *Dhammasaṅgaṇī* is essentially a book of classifications and definitions, while the sixth book of the Abhidhamma, the *Yamaka*, develops a very elaborate and cautious delimitation of terms that might appear even too labored and elaborate for our sensibility.

Since the suttas principally serve as a source of guidance for the actual daily life of the disciple, they are generally expressed in terms of conventional language (*vohāra-vacana*), making reference to persons and personal attributes. In the Abhidhamma, however, this sutta terminology is replaced by a more philosophically precise terminology, which accords with the egoless or "impersonal" and ever-changing nature of actuality. The Abhidhamma texts use this terminology, true in the strict or "highest sense" (*paramattha*), to explain in detail the main tenets of the Dhamma.

While vague definitions and loosely used terms are like blunt tools unfit to do the work they are meant for, and while concepts based on wrong notions will necessarily beg the question to be scrutinized and will thus prejudice the issue, the use of appropriate and carefully tempered conceptual tools is an indispensable condition for success in the quest for liberating knowledge. Hence the fact that Abhidhamma literature is a rich source of exact terminology is a feature not to be underestimated.

Analysis of Consciousness

One of the Abhidhamma's chief contributions to human thought is, as we have already intimated, the analysis and classification of consciousness, a project undertaken in the first part of the *Dhammasaṅgaṇī*. Here, for the first time in history, the human mind, so evanescent and elusive, has been subjected to a comprehensive, thorough, and unprejudiced scrutiny. The approach taken is one of a rigorous phenomenology that disposes of the notion that any kind of static unity or underlying substance can be traced in the mind. However, the basic ethical layout and soteriological purpose of this psychology effectively prevents its realistic, unmetaphysical analysis of the mind from implying conclusions of ethical materialism or theoretical and practical amoralism.

The method of investigation applied in the Abhidhamma is *inductive*, being based exclusively on an unprejudiced and subtle introspective observation of mental processes. The procedure used in the *Dhammasaṅgaṇī* for the analysis of consciousness is precisely that postulated by Whitehead: "It is impossible to over-emphasize the point that the key to the process of induction, as used either in science or in our ordinary life, is to be found in the right understanding of the immediate occasion of knowledge in its full concreteness.... In any occasion of cognition, that which is known is an actual occasion of experience, as diversified by reference to a realm of entities which transcend that immediate occasion in that they have analogous or different connections with other occasions of experience."[10]

Whitehead's term "occasion" corresponds to the Abhidhammic concept *samaya* (time, occasion, conjunction of circumstances), which occurs in all principal paragraphs of the *Dhammasaṅgaṇī*, and there denotes the starting point of the analysis. The term receives a detailed and very instructive treatment in its commentary, the *Atthasālinī*.

The Buddha succeeded in reducing this "immediate occasion" of an act of cognition to a single moment of consciousness, which, however, in its subtlety and evanescence cannot be observed, directly and separately, by a mind untrained in introspective meditation. Just as the minute living beings in the microcosm of a drop of water become visible only through a microscope, so too the exceedingly short-lived processes in the world of the mind become cognizable only with the help of a very subtle instrument of mental scrutiny—a mind sharpened by methodical meditative training. None but the kind of introspective mindfulness or attention (*sati*) that has acquired, in meditative absorption, a high degree of inner equipoise, purity, and firmness (*upekkhā-sati-pārisuddhi*), will possess the keenness, subtlety, and speed of cognitive response required for such delicate mental microscopy. Without such meditative preparation the only means of research open to the investigator will be inference from comparisons between various complete or fragmentary series of thought-moments. But if cautious and intelligent use is made of one's own introspective observations and of the treatment of meditative experience found in the suttas and Abhidhamma, even this approach, though far from infallible, may well lead to important and reliable conclusions.

The *Anupada Sutta* (*MN* No. 111) reports that the Venerable Sāriputta, after rising from meditative absorption (*jhāna*), was able to analyze each meditative attainment into its constituent mental factors. This may be regarded as a precursor of the more detailed analysis given in the *Dhammasaṅgaṇī.*

The *Milindapañha* ("The Questions of King Milinda"), too, with fitting similes, emphasizes the difficulty of analyzing the mental process and the greatness of the Buddha's achievement in making such an analysis:

> "A difficult feat indeed was accomplished, great king, by the Exalted One."
>
> "Which is that difficult feat, Venerable Nāgasena?"
>
> "The Exalted One, great king, has accomplished a difficult task when he analyzed a mental process having a single object, as consisting of consciousness with its concomitants, as follows: 'This is sense-contact, this is feeling, perception, volition, consciousness.'"
>
> "Give an illustration of it, venerable sir."
>
> "Suppose, great king, a man has gone to the sea by boat and takes with the hollow of his hand a little sea water and tastes it. Will this man know, 'This is water from the Ganges, this is water from such other rivers as the Yamunā, the Aciravatī, etc.'?"
>
> "He can hardly know that."

"But a still more difficult task, great king, was accomplished by the Exalted One when he analyzed a mental process having a single object, as consisting of consciousness with its concomitants."[11]

The rather terse and abstract form in which the *Dhammasaṅgaṇī* presents its analysis of the mind should not mislead us into supposing that it is a product of late scholastic thought. When, in the course of closer study, we notice the admirable inner consistency of the system, and gradually become aware of many of its subtle conceptions and far-reaching implications, we will be convinced that at least the fundamental outlines and the key notes of Abhidhamma psychology must be the result of a profound intuition gained through direct and penetrative introspection. It will appear increasingly unlikely that the essential framework of the Abhidhamma could be the product of a cumbersome process of discursive thinking and artificial thought construction. This impression of the essentially intuitive origin of the Abhidhamma's mind-doctrine will also strengthen our conviction that the basic structural principles of the *Dhammasaṅgaṇī* and the *Paṭṭhāna* must be ascribed to the Buddha himself and his great disciples. What is called "scholastic thought"—which has its merit in its own sphere and does not deserve wholesale condemnation—may have had its share later in formulating, elaborating, and codifying the teachings originally sprung from intuitive insight.

If we turn from the Abhidhamma to the highest contemporary achievements of non-Buddhist Indian thought in the field of mind and "soul," i.e., the early Upanishads and Sāṁkhya, we would find that apart from single great intuitions, they teem with concepts derived from mythology, ritual, and abstract speculation. In comparison the realistic, sober, and scientific spirit of the Abhidhamma psychology (as well as its nucleus found in the suttas) stands out very strongly. For those who could appreciate the significance of this contrast, the Abhidhamma would have inspired especially high esteem and admiration. But even if the Abhidhamma psychology is compared with later psychological teachings of the East and the West, its distance from almost all of them remains fundamentally the same; for only the

Buddha's teaching on mind keeps entirely free from the notions of self, ego, soul, or any other permanent entity in or behind the mind.

THE DOCTRINE OF NON-SELF

It is on this very doctrine of non-self, or *anattā,* that all Abhidhamma thought converges, and this is where it culminates. The elaborate and thorough treatment of *anattā* is also the most important *practical* contribution that the Abhidhamma makes to the progress of the Buddhist disciple toward liberation. The Abhidhamma provides ample material for meditation in the field of insight (*vipassanā*) concerning impermanence and selflessness, and this material has been analyzed down to the subtlest point and is couched in strictly philosophical language.

There will certainly be many for whom the degree of analytical detail found in the Sutta Piṭaka will be enough to understand *anattā,* and to serve as a guideline in meditative practice. But there are also minds that require repeated and varied demonstration and illustration of a truth before they are entirely satisfied and convinced. There are also others who wish to push their analysis to the greatest detail possible and to extend it to the very smallest unit accessible, in order to make quite sure that even the realm of the infinitesimal, of the material and psychical "atoms," does not hide any self or abiding substance. To such minds the Abhidhamma will be of great value. But also those who are generally satisfied with the expositions in the suttas may sometimes wish to investigate more closely a particular point that has roused their interest or that presents difficulties. To them too the Abhidhamma will prove helpful.

Besides helping such individual cases, study of the Abhidhamma will more broadly assist in the slow, difficult change of outlook from the viewpoint of "self" to that of "non-self." Once one has grasped intellectually the doctrine of non-self, one can certainly succeed in applying it to theoretical and practical issues if only one remembers it in time and deliberately directs one's thoughts and volitions accordingly. But except for such deliberate directing of thought, which in most cases will be relatively rare, the mind will continue to move in the old-accustomed ruts of "I" and "mine," "self" and "substance," which are deeply ingrained in our daily language and our modes of thinking; and our actions too will still continue to be frequently governed by our ancient egocentric impulses. An occasional intellectual assent to the true outlook of *anattā* will not effect great changes in that situation. The only remedy is for bad or wrong habits of action, speech, and thought to be gradually replaced by good and correct habits until the latter become as spontaneous as the former are now. It is therefore necessary that right thinking, that is, thinking in terms of *anattā*, be made the subject of regular and systematic mental training until the power of wrong habits of thought is reduced and finally broken. The Abhidhamma in general, and in particular the various triads and dyads of terms as listed in the *mātikā*, the "matrix" of the Abhidhamma Piṭaka, provide ample material for such "fluency exercises" of right thinking. Familiarity with the application of the "impersonal" viewpoint of the Abhidhamma and with the terminology by which it is expressed will exercise a considerable formative influence on the mind.

Abhidhamma and Meditation

A fertile soil for the origin and persistence of beliefs and ideas about a self, soul, God, or any other form of an absolute entity, is *misinterpreted meditative experience* occurring in devotional rapture or mystical trance. Such experience is generally interpreted by the mystic or theologian as the revelation of a God, or union with some divine principle, or the manifestation of our true and eternal self. Such interpretations are conceived and accepted all the more readily since such meditative experience so greatly transcends the average level of consciousness that the contemplative is readily tempted to connect it with a deity or some other eternal principle. The overwhelming impact of such meditative experience on the mind will produce a strong conviction of its reality and superiority; and this strong feeling of assurance will be extended to the theological or speculative interpretation too. In that way these interpretations will obtain a strong hold on the mind; for they are imagined to correspond with actual, irrefutable experience, when in fact they are only superimpositions on the latter.

The analytical method of the Abhidhamma gives immunity against such deceptive interpretations. In the *Dhammasaṅgaṇī* the consciousness of *jhāna*, meditative absorption, is subjected to the same sober analysis as the ordinary states of mind. It is shown that meditative consciousness, too, is a transitory combination of impermanent, conditioned, and impersonal mental factors, which differ from their counterparts accompanying ordinary consciousness only in their greater intensity and purity. They thus do not warrant any assumption of a divine manifestation or an eternal self. It has already been mentioned how the Venerable Sāriputta undertook such an analysis of his meditative experience.

It is characteristic of the spirit of the Buddha's Teaching that the disciple is always advised to follow up his or her meditative absorption by an analytical retrospection (*paccavekkhaṇa*) on the mental states just experienced, comprehending them by insight (*vipassanā*) as impersonal and evanescent, and therefore not to be adhered to. By so doing, three main mental defilements (*kilesa*) are effectively warded off, which otherwise may easily arise as a consequence of the overwhelming impact that the meditative experience might make on the mind: (1) craving (*taṇhā*) for these experiences, clinging to them, and longing for them for their own sake (*jhāna-nikanti*, "indulgence in jhāna"); (2) the false view (*diṭṭhi*) that these meditative experiences imply a self or a deity; and (3) the conceit (*māna*) that may arise through having attained these exalted states.

These remarks refer to the division of Buddhist meditation called "development of tranquillity" (*samatha-bhāvanā*), aiming at the attainment of jhāna. Turning now to the "development of insight" (*vipassanā-bhāvanā*), the classificatory terms of the Abhidhamma *mātikā*, as explained in the *Dhammasaṅgaṇī*, etc., provide numerous possibilities for including in them the various particular subjects of insight. By such reference to the triads or dyads of terms in the *mātikā* a limited subject of insight can easily be connected with the entire world of actuality, thereby enriching its significance. Such a particular subject of insight may either be deliberately chosen from the traditional subjects of meditation or may consist in some incidental occurrence in life. The latter again may be either some deeply stirring inner or outer experience or even a quite ordinary happening of everyday life taken as an object of right mindfulness and clear comprehension (*sati-sampajañña*), as is often reported of meditating monks and nuns of old. If that event can at once be referred to one of the triads or dyads of Abhidhammic terms, which comprise the whole of actuality, the impulses it sets off can be more effectively channeled toward deep religious commotion (*saṁvega*) and insight. Thus a single act of penetrative understanding starting from a limited object may acquire such intensity, width, and depth as to either lead to, or effectively prepare for, liberating insight. This accords with what a great Buddhist thinker has said: "The understanding of one single thing means the understanding of all; the voidness of one single thing is the voidness of all."[12]

Abhidhamma and the Dhamma Teacher

We have seen how important a study of the Abhidhamma can be for clarity of thought, for correct understanding, and for personal spiritual development. Yet, while a detailed knowledge of Abhidhamma philosophy might well be optional for those devoted exclusively to meditation, it is different for those who wish to teach and explain the Dhamma to others. Here the Theravāda tradition considers familiarity with the Abhidhamma, even in its details, an indispensable qualification. We read (*Asl* 29): "Only monks who are proficient in Abhidhamma can be regarded as 'preachers of Dhamma' (*dhammakathika*). Others, even if they actually engage in preaching, cannot truly be so called. When giving a doctrinal exposition, they may, for instance, mix up the various kinds of kamma and kammic results or the various factors found when analyzing body and mind. But those proficient in Abhidhamma do not make such mistakes."

Features that make the Abhidhamma so important for teachers of the Dhamma are especially these: its systematic organization of the doctrinal material contained in the Sutta Piṭaka; its use of orderly and methodical thinking; its precise definitions of technical terms and delimitation of their referents; its treatment of various subjects and life situations from the viewpoint of ultimate truth (*paramattha*); its mastery of doctrinal detail.

The Evaluation and Authenticity of Abhidhamma

Even in the ancient past opinions about the Abhidhamma Piṭaka ranged between the extremes of unquestioning veneration and wholesale rejection. Very soon after the Abhidhamma became ascendant, there were teachers who questioned the claim that the Abhidhamma Piṭaka could be regarded as the genuine word of the Buddha. The early sect of the Sautrāntikas, as their name indicates, regarded only the Sutta and Vinaya Piṭakas as canonical but not the Abhidhamma.

It may have been a follower of that sect who is depicted criticizing the Abhidhamma lecture of a monk thus (*Asl* 28):

> "You have quoted, O preacher, a long sutta that seems to girdle Mount Meru. What is the name of it?"
> "It is an Abhidhamma sutta."
> "But why did you quote an Abhidhamma sutta? Is it not befitting to cite a sutta that has been proclaimed by the Buddha?"
> "And by whom do you think the Abhidhamma was proclaimed?"
> "It was not proclaimed by the Buddha."

Thereupon that monk is severely rebuked by the preacher, and after that the text continues (*Asl* 29):

> One who excludes the Abhidhamma (from the Buddha-Word) damages the Conqueror's Wheel of Dhamma (*jinacakkaṁ pahāraṁ deti*). He excludes thereby the omniscience of the Tathāgata and impoverishes the grounds of the Master's knowledge of self-confidence (*vesārajja-ñāṇa*, to which omniscience belongs); he deceives an audience anxious to learn; he obstructs (progress to) the noble paths

> of holiness; he makes all the eighteen causes of discord appear at once. By so doing he deserves the disciplinary punishment of temporary segregation, or the reproof of the assembly of monks.

This very severe attitude seems somewhat extreme, but it may be explained as a defensive reaction against sectarian tendencies at that period.

The main arguments of Theravāda against those who deny the authenticity of the Abhidhamma are stated in the *Atthasālinī* as follows:

1. The Buddha has to be regarded as the first Ābhidhammika, because, "he had already penetrated the Abhidhamma when sitting under the Bodhi Tree" (*Asl* 17).

2. "The Abhidhamma, the ultimate doctrine, is the domain of omniscient Buddhas only, not the domain of others.... These profound teachings are unmistakably the property of an enlightened being, a Buddha. To deny this is as senseless as stealing the horse of a World Ruler, unique in its excellence, or any other possession of his, and showing oneself in public with it. And why? Because they obviously belong to and befit a king" (*Asl* 29–30).

Even to non-Buddhists, who do not regard the Buddha as an omniscient one but simply as a great and profound thinker, it would seem improbable that he would have remained unaware of the philosophical and psychological implications of his teachings, even if he did not speak of them at the very start and to all his followers. Considering the undeniable profundity of the Abhidhamma, the worldwide horizons of that gigantic system, and the inexhaustible impulses to thought that it offers—in view of all this it seems much more probable that at least the basic teachings of the Abhidhamma derive from that highest intuition that the Buddha calls *sammā sambodhi,* perfect enlightenment. It appears therefore quite plausible when the old Theravāda tradition ascribes the framework and fundamental intuitions of the Abhidhamma—and no more than that—to the Master himself. A quite different question, of course, is the origin of the codified Abhidhamma literature as we have it at present. But this problem cannot be dealt with here, and in any case the sources and facts at our disposal do not allow definite conclusions to be drawn.

The Theravāda tradition holds that the Buddha first preached the Abhidhamma in the Tāvatiṁsa heaven to the gods who had assembled from ten thousand world systems.[13] The preaching continued for the three-month period of the rains retreat. Each day, when he returned to the human world for his meal, he conveyed the bare method to the elder Sāriputta. Whatever one may think about this tradition—whether, like the devout Asian Buddhist, one regards it as a historical account, or whether one takes it as a significant legend—one fact emerges from it fairly clearly: the originators of this very early tradition did not think the Abhidhamma texts had been literally expounded by the Buddha to human beings in the same way that he expounded the suttas. If one wishes to give a psychological interpretation to the traditional account, one might say that the sojourn in the world of the gods refers to periods of intense contemplation transcending the reaches of an earthbound mentality; and that from the heights of such contemplation the Master brought the fundamental teachings back to the world of normal human consciousness and transmitted them to philosophically gifted disciples like Sāriputta.

In a comparative evaluation of the Abhidhamma and the suttas, the fact is often overlooked—which, however, has been repeatedly stressed by the Venerable Nyanatiloka Mahāthera—that the Sutta Piṭaka too contains a considerable amount of pure Abhidhamma. This comprises all those numerous texts expounded from the ultimate standpoint (*paramattha*), which make use of strict philosophical terminology and explain experience in terms of selfless, conditioned processes; for example, those suttas dealing with the five aggregates, the eighteen elements, and the twelve sense bases (*khandha, dhātu, āyatana*).

One also frequently hears the question asked whether a knowledge of the Abhidhamma is necessary for a full understanding of the Dhamma or for final liberation. In this general form, the question is not quite adequately put. Even in the Sutta Piṭaka many different approaches and methods of practice are offered as "gates" to the understanding of the same Four Noble Truths. Not all of them are "necessary" for reaching the final goal, Nibbāna, nor are all suitable in their entirety for every individual disciple. Rather, the Buddha taught a variety of approaches and left it to the disciples to make their personal choices among them, according to their personal circumstances, inclination, and level of maturity.

The same holds true for the Abhidhamma both as a whole and in its single aspects and teachings. Perhaps the best explanation of the relationship between the Abhidhamma and the suttas is a pair of similes given in a conversation by the Venerable Pëlëne Vajirañāṇa Mahāthera, the founding prelate of the Vajirārāma Monastery in Colombo: "The Abhidhamma is like a powerful magnifying glass, but the understanding gained from the suttas is the eye itself, which performs the act of seeing. Or the Abhidhamma is like a medicine container with a label giving an exact analysis of the medicine; but the knowledge gained from the suttas is the medicine itself, which alone is able to cure the illness and its symptoms."

Concluding Remarks and a Warning

Taking a middle path between overrating or underrating the Abhidhamma, we might say: The teachings in the Sutta Piṭaka with an Abhidhamma flavor—that is, those given in precise philosophical terminology—are certainly indispensable for the understanding and practice of the Dhamma; and the elaboration of these teachings in the Abhidhamma proper may prove very helpful, and in some cases even necessary, for both understanding and practice. As to the codified Abhidhamma Piṭaka, familiarity with all its details is certainly not compulsory; but if it is studied and applied in the way briefly indicated in these pages, this will surely nurture a true understanding of actuality and aid the work of practice aimed at liberation. Also, if suitably presented, the Abhidhamma can provide those with a philosophical bent a stimulating approach to the Dhamma that could prove fruitful, provided they take care to balance intellectual understanding with actual practice. Such an approach to the Dhamma should certainly not be blocked by the wholesale disparagement of Abhidhamma study sometimes found nowadays among Buddhists in the West, and even in Asia. Dangers of one-sided emphasis and development lurk not only in the Abhidhamma but also in other approaches to the Dhamma, and they cannot be entirely avoided until a very high level of harmonious integration of the spiritual faculties has been attained.

To be sure, without an earnest attempt to apply the Abhidhamma teachings in such ways as intimated above, they may easily become a rigid system of lifeless concepts. Like other philosophical systems, the Abhidhamma can lead to a dogmatic and superstitious belief in words, for example, to the opinion that one really knows something about a subject if one is skilled in navigating its conceptual system. The study of the Abhidhamma should therefore not be allowed to degenerate into a mere collecting, counting, and arranging of such conceptual labels. This would make of Abhidhamma study—though, of course, not of the Abhidhamma itself—just one more among the many intellectual "playthings" that serve as an escape from facing reality, or as a "respectable excuse" with which to evade the hard inner work needed for liberation. A merely abstract and conceptual approach to the Abhidhamma may also lead to that kind of intellectual pride that often goes together with specialized knowledge.

If these pitfalls are avoided, there is a good chance that the Abhidhamma may again become a living force that stimulates thought and aids the meditative endeavor for the mind's liberation, the purpose for which the Abhidhamma is really meant. To achieve this, however, the Abhidhamma teachings must be not merely accepted and transmitted verbally but carefully examined and contemplated in their philosophical and practical implications. These teachings are often extremely condensed, and on many points of interest even the classical commentaries are silent. Thus to work out their implications will require the devoted effort of searching and imaginative minds. As they will have to work on neglected and difficult ground, they should not lack the courage to make initial mistakes, which can be rectified by discussion and constant reference to the teachings of the Sutta Piṭaka.

II

The Twofold Method of Abhidhamma Philosophy

Having used the term "Abhidhamma philosophy" in the title of this chapter, we must first state in what sense these two words are to be taken here.

It is well known that the Abhidhamma Piṭaka forms the third main division of the Pāli Canon and consists of seven books. But when speaking in these pages of the Abhidhamma in general we have in mind particularly the first and last of these seven books, namely, the *Dhammasaṅgaṇī* and the *Paṭṭhāna*, which are aptly characterized by the Venerable Nyanatiloka as "the quintessence of the entire Abhidhamma."[14]

Now, in what sense can the Abhidhamma be called a philosophy? Let us make a rough division of philosophy into phenomenology and ontology, and briefly characterize them as follows: *Phenomenology* deals, as the name implies, with "phenomena," that is, with the world of internal and external experience. *Ontology*, or metaphysics, inquires into the existence and nature of an essence, or ultimate principle, underlying the phenomenal world. In other words, *phenomenology* investigates the questions: *What* happens in the world of our experience? *How* does it happen? Of course, when inquiring into the "what" and "how," philosophy is not satisfied with the surface view of reality as it presents itself to the naive and uncritical mind. *Ontology*, on the other hand, insists, at least in most of its systems, that the question "how" cannot be answered without reference to an eternal essence behind reality, whether conceived as immanent or transcendent. Particularly in the latter case the question "how" is frequently changed into a "why," containing the tacit assumption that the answer has to be sought somewhere or somehow outside of the given reality.

The Abhidhamma doubtlessly belongs to the first of these two divisions of philosophy, that is, to phenomenology. Even that fundamental Abhidhamma term *dhamma*, which includes corporeal as well as mental "things," may well be rendered by "phenomena"[15]—if only we keep in mind that in Abhidhammic usage "phenomenon" must not be thought to imply a correlative "noumenon" as, for instance, in Kant's philosophy.

In describing the Abhidhamma as phenomenology we must make two reservations, which however will not greatly alter the substance of our statement. First, Nibbāna, mostly under the name *asaṅkhatā dhātu* ("the unconditioned element"), also appears in the "Enumeration of Phenomena" (*Dhammasaṅgaṇī*) in several of the classificatory groups treated in that work. Being "supramundane" (*lokuttara*), Nibbāna is certainly, in the sense of the term *lokuttara*, a metaphysical or transcendent entity. The latter term "transcendent" may well be rendered by another Abhidhammic classification of Nibbāna, *apariyāpanna*, that is, "not included" in the three realms of conditioned existence conceived by Buddhism.[16] Though Nibbāna, as the *asaṅkhatā dhātu*, does in fact appear quite often in the *Dhammasaṅgaṇī*, it should be noted that: (1) in all cases it is merely mentioned without any further explanation beyond the classificatory heading under which it appears, and so it differs in that respect from the other "things," to all of which a definition is added; (2) the classifications of Nibbāna are all negative in character.[17] On the other hand it is noteworthy that Nibbāna is definitely termed a *dhamma*, even in classifications where it cannot be viewed as an object of thought (that is, a *dhamma* in the sense of a mental object, correlated to *mano,* mind). So we have to admit that this sole *nonphenomenal* entity belongs likewise to the system of the Abhidhamma, but—and this reinforces our point—it is never enlarged upon because Nibbāna is an object of realization and not of philosophical research.

Our second reservation with regard to an exclusively phenomenological view of the Abhidhamma is this: The penetrative phenomenological investigation undertaken in the Abhidhamma makes a definite and valuable contribution to ontological problems, that is, to the search for an abiding essence in reality. The Abhidhamma philosophy shows clearly and irrefutably where such an alleged essence can never be found, namely, anywhere in the world of the five aggregates (*khandha*). The most sublime states of meditative consciousness—so frequently identified with the manifestation of, or the mystical union with, a deity of a personal or impersonal nature—are included in those five phenomenal objects of clinging (*upādānakkhandha*) and excluded from the sphere of the unconditioned element. At the same time, the thorough analysis of all phenomena undertaken in the Abhidhamma leaves no doubt as to what Nibbāna definitely *is not.* It is true that these ontological results of the Abhidhamma are "merely negative," but they certainly represent more substantial and consequential contributions to the ontological problem than the "positive" assertions of many metaphysical systems, indulging in unprovable or fallacious conceptual speculations.

Having dealt with these two reservations, we may return to our initial simplified statement and formulate it now in this way: *The Abhidhamma is not a speculative but a descriptive philosophy.*

For the purpose of describing phenomena, the Abhidhamma uses two complementary methods: that of analysis, and that of investigating the relations (or the conditionality) of things. Both these typical features of the Abhidhamma, that is, the limitation to a purely descriptive procedure and the twofold method, will become evident if we glance at the fundamental schemata of the two principal books of the Abhidhamma mentioned above.

1. In its chapter on consciousness, the analytical *Dhammasaṅgaṇī,* or "Enumeration of Phenomena," has the following descriptive pattern: "At a time when (such or such a type of) consciousness has arisen, at that time there exist the following phenomena..."[18]

2. The *Paṭṭhāna,* or "Book of Origination," the principal work dealing with the Buddhist philosophy of relations, uses the following basic formula: "Dependent on a (wholesome) phenomenon there may arise a (wholesome) phenomenon, conditioned by way of (root-cause)."

It is evident from the very wording that in both cases the statements made are purely descriptive. In the first case a description is given of what is really happening when we say "consciousness has arisen," that is to say, what are the constituents of that event which is seemingly of a unitary, noncomposite nature. In the second case, the description answers the question *how*, that is, under what conditions the event is happening.

The mere juxtaposition of these two basic schemata of the Abhidhamma already allows us to formulate an important axiom of Buddhist philosophy: *A complete description of a thing requires, besides its analysis, also a statement of its relations to other things.*

Though the Abhidhamma, being nonmetaphysical, does not deal with any Beyond as to things in general (*meta ta physika*), it nevertheless does go beyond *single* things, that is, beyond things artificially isolated for the purpose of analytical description. The connection or relation between things, that is, their conditionality (*idappaccayatā*), is dealt with particularly in the *Paṭṭhāna*, which supplies a vast net of conditional relations obtaining between the conditioning phenomena and the things they condition. But the mere fact of relational existence is already implicit in the thorough analysis undertaken in the *Dhammasaṅgaṇī*, where it is shown that even the smallest psychic unit, that is, a single moment of consciousness, is constituted by a multiplicity of active mental factors bound together in a relationship of interdependence. This fact is frequently emphasized in the *Atthasālinī*. For example, when commenting on the formula for the first type of wholesome consciousness in the *Dhammasaṅgaṇī* (see below, p. 31), the *Atthasālinī* (pp. 58–59) enumerates the different meanings that the word *samaya* ("time" or "occasion") may have in this context. One of these meanings is *samūha*, aggregation (or constellation) of things, and if *samaya* is understood thus, the formula would read: "In whichever aggregation of things a wholesome state of consciousness... has arisen, in that aggregation exist: sense-contact, etc." Here the commentator remarks: "Thereby (that is, by the above explanation of *samaya*) the view is rejected that any one thing may arise singly" (*Asl* 59). In other words: thorough analysis implies an acknowledgment of relationship. Two more axioms in the same text (*Asl* 59–61) stress the need to investigate the relations of things: "Nothing arises from a single cause" (*ekakāraṇavādo paṭisedhito hoti*); and "Nothing exists (or moves) by its own power" (*dhammānaṁ savasavattitābhimāno paṭisedhito hoti*).[19]

We can add as third the already quoted sentence in an abbreviated form: "Nothing arises singly" (ekass' eva dhammassa uppatti paṭisedhito hoti).

These terse sentences represent three fundamental principles of Buddhist philosophy, which well deserve to be taken out of the mass of expository detail where they easily escape the attention they merit. Next to the fact of impermanence (*aniccatā*), these three axioms, implying as they do the principle of conditionality (*idappaccayatā*), are the main supports for the fundamental Buddhist doctrine of non-self or unsubstantiality (*anattā*).

The analysis as undertaken in the *Dhammasaṅgaṇī* shows that the smallest accessible psychic unit, a moment of consciousness, is as little indivisible (*atomos*), uniform, and undifferentiated as the material atom of modern physics. Like the physical atom, a moment of consciousness is a correlational system of its factors, functions, energies, or aspects, or whatever other name we choose to give to the "components" of that hypothetical psychic unit. In the Abhidhamma these "components" are called simply *dhammā*, that is, "things" or "states."

It should be noted, however, that the *Paṭṭhāna*, the principal work of Buddhist "conditionalism," is not so much concerned with the relations within a single psychic unit (*cittakkhaṇa*)—which we shall call "internal relations"—as with the connections between several such units. But these "external relations" are to a great extent dependent on the "internal relations" of the given single unit or of previous ones, that is, on the modes of combination and the relative strength of the different mental factors within a single moment of consciousness. This shows that the analytical method is as important for the relational one as the latter is for the former.

The presence or absence, strength or weakness, of a certain mental factor (*dhamma* or *cetasika*) may decide the occurrence or nonoccurrence of a given external relation. For example, in any wholesome state of consciousness the mental factor of energy (*viriya*) functions as right effort (*sammā-vāyāma*), the sixth factor of the Noble Eightfold Path. Even though this state of consciousness may be one dissociated from knowledge, the presence of energy, one of the path factors, may establish a relationship with a future state of consciousness where the path factor "right view" (*sammā-diṭṭhi*) is also present. In other words, the tendency toward liberation inherent in the path factors is, in our example, at first mainly expressed by the factor "energy," that is, the active wish and endeavor directed to liberation. This energy naturally strives to acquire all the other requisites for reaching the goal, particularly the path factor of right view. If there is the definite awareness that a certain quality of mind or character is a member of a group of factors sharing a common purpose, then the respective state of consciousness will naturally tend to complete that group either by acquiring the missing members or by strengthening those that are undeveloped. Thereby a bridge is built to another type of consciousness. Thus, from this example, we can see how the composition of a state of consciousness—its internal relations—influences its external relations.

As already mentioned, the *Paṭṭhāna* investigates only the external relations, but in another work of the Abhidhamma, the *Vibhaṅga*, the internal relations too are treated. In the *Paccayākāra-vibhaṅga,* the "Treatise on the Modes of Conditionality," the schema of the *Dhammasaṅgaṇī* is combined with the formula of dependent origination (*paṭicca-samuppāda*); for example: "(At a time when the first unwholesome state of consciousness has arisen), there arises dependent on ignorance the (respective) kamma formation (*avijjāpaccayā saṅkhāro,* in singular!)." In that text, there are some deviations from the normal formula of dependent origination, varying in accordance with the type of consciousness in question. This remarkable application of the *paṭicca-samuppāda* is called in the commentary *ekacittakkhaṇika-paṭicca-samuppāda,* that is, "dependent origination within a single moment of consciousness." The commentary indicates which of the twenty-four modes of conditionality (*paccaya*) are applicable to which links of that "momentary" *paṭicca-samuppāda.* In this way, by showing that even an infinitesimally brief moment of consciousness is actually an intricate net of relations, the erroneous belief in a static world is attacked and destroyed at its root. In that important but much too little known chapter of the *Vibhaṅga,* both methods of the Abhidhamma, the analytical and the relational, are exemplified and harmonized simultaneously.[20]

The Buddha, who is so rightly called "skillful in his method of instruction" (*nayakusalo*), has on other occasions, too, used the same ingenious approach of first applying separately two different methods and afterwards combining them. Here are only a few examples:

According to the *Satipaṭṭhāna Sutta* (*DN* No. 22; *MN* No. 10), the contemplation of different objects should proceed in two phases:

Phase I:

1. *ajjhatta,* the contemplation of phenomena (corporeal and mental) as appearing in oneself
2. *bahiddhā,* phenomena appearing in others
3. *ajjhatta-bahiddhā,* the combination of both

Here the synthetical or relational method is applied by breaking down wrong differentiations between ego and non-ego and by showing that the life process is an impersonal continuum. Only a thorough practice of the first two stages will lead to the result.

Phase II:

1. *samudayadhamma,* phenomena viewed as arising
2. *vayadhamma,* phenomena viewed as passing away
3. *samudaya-vayadhamma,* the combination of both

Here the analytical method is applied in order to break up wrong identifications.

In the course of the practice of *satipaṭṭhāna,* both partial aspects, the synthetical and the analytical (Phases I and II), gradually merge into one perfect and undivided "vision of things as they really are."

The following instruction for the graduated practice of insight (*vipassanā*), frequently given in the commentaries and the *Visuddhimagga,* follows a similar method:

1. analysis of the corporeal (*rūpa*)
2. analysis of the mental (*nāma*)
3. contemplation of both (*nāma rūpa*)
4. both viewed as conditioned (*sappaccaya*)
5. application of the three characteristics to mind-and-body and their conditions[21]

Only the application of both methods—the analytical and the synthetical—can produce a full and correct understanding of the egolessness (*anattā*) and insubstantiality (*suññatā*) of all phenomena. A one-sided application of analysis may easily result in the view of a rigid world of material and psychic atoms. When science has come close to the Buddhist *anattā*-doctrine, it has done so (at least up to the beginning of this century) mostly through a radical application of the analytical method, so its kinship to the Buddhist concept is only a partial one and has to be accepted with reservations. However, this analytical approach of science has been supplemented by the dynamic worldview that dominates the latest trends in modern physics, psychology, and philosophy.

To be fair, we have to admit that even distinguished Buddhist writers of the past, and of our time as well, have not always avoided the pitfalls of a one-sided analytical approach. This may easily happen because analysis takes a very prominent place in Buddhist philosophy and meditation. Furthermore, in striving for insight, that is, for a "vision of things as they really are," analysis comes first. The first task is to remove by analysis the basis for all the numerous false notions of substantial unities, such as the unquestioned belief of the average person in an identical ego, or theological faith in an individual soul, or the various concepts of materialist or idealist systems. Finally, analysis tends to be overemphasized in expositions of the Abhidhamma because the analytical *Dhammasaṅgaṇī* makes relatively easier reading than the *Paṭṭhāna*, giving more concrete facts than the latter book. The *Paṭṭhāna* furnishes only an abstract scheme of all possible relations scantily illustrated. It deals with the formal aspect of the life process. The "bodies" within which these abstract principles operate are supplied in the analytical books of the Abhidhamma. In other words, analysis describes, by critically chosen terms, the "things" that actually enter into those relations dealt with by the synthetical method. All these points are strong temptations to stress unduly the analytical aspect of the Abhidhamma philosophy.

So it is all the more imperative to supplement the analytical aspect by constant awareness of the fact that the "things" presented by analysis are never isolated, self-contained units but are conditioned and conditioning events, as is emphasized by the commentarial axioms cited above. They occur only in temporary aggregations or combinations that are constantly in a process of formation and dissolution. But the word "dissolution" does not imply the complete disappearance of all the components of the respective aggregation. Some of them always "survive"—or, more correctly, recur—in the combination of the next moment, while others, conditioned by their previous occurrence, may reappear much later. Thus the flux of the life stream is preserved uninterrupted.

Bare analysis starts, or pretends to start, its investigations by selecting single objects existing in the sector of time called "the present." The present is certainly the only reality concretely existing, but it is a very elusive reality that is constantly on the move from an unreal future to an unreal past. Indeed, strictly speaking, the object of analysis, at the time it is taken up for examination, already belongs to the past, not to the present. This is stated by the commentators of old: "Just as it is impossible to touch with one's fingertip that very same fingertip, so too the arising, continuing, and ceasing of a thought cannot be known by the same thought."[22] Apart from the so-called "momentary present" (*khaṇa-paccuppanna*), which consists of a single virtually imperceptible moment of consciousness, the statement that, strictly speaking, a thought has not a present but a past object holds good even if we have in mind the much wider "serial present" (*santati-paccuppanna*), that is, the perceptible sequence of several moments of consciousness, which alone is actually experienced as present. To a philosophical mind, the duration of the object of bare analysis in an artificially delimited, elusive, and not even genuine present lends to it a strangely illusory character, which contrasts quaintly with the frequent assertion of "pure analysts" that they alone deal with "real facts." Indeed, these "hard facts" are constantly slipping through their fingers! A frequent and vivid experience and contemplation of that illusory nature of the present, not in the well-known general sense but as established by Abhidhammic analysis, will greatly help in the final understanding of *suññatā*, that is, voidness or insubstantiality.

We have noted how bare analysis starts with single objects occurring in the present. But even the most complacent analysts cannot afford to stop at that point. They must take into account the fact that other "single" objects existing in the "same" space-time act upon their original object, and are in turn acted upon by it. They also have to note that the object chosen undergoes, even before their eyes, a series of consecutive changes. In view of these considerations, analysis must renounce its self-sufficiency and admit within its range of scrutiny at least those two facts of relational existence and constant change. When that is done we must now speak of "qualified analysis," as distinct from the previous "bare analysis." In its widened scope, "qualified analysis" spreads, as it were, its objects and the results of its investigations over a plane or surface with only the two dimensions of breadth and length. The "breadth" consists in the first-mentioned relational fact: the coexistence of other phenomena insofar as they are in interconnection with the original object of analysis. The "length" signifies the second relational fact: the sequence of observed, consecutive changes stretching forward in time. Thus qualified analysis takes into consideration only those of the twenty-four modes of conditionality treated in the *Paṭṭhāna* that refer to coexistence (e.g., *sahajāta-paccaya,* "conascence") or to linear sequence (e.g., *anantara-paccaya,* "contiguity").

Both bare and qualified analysis are closely bound to a spatial view of the world and, as we have seen, to a limited two-dimensional space. Those who rely on these two kinds of analysis fear nothing so much as the disturbing intrusion of the time factor into their well-ordered but static, sham world of supposedly "unambiguous and palpable facts." Having had to admit the time factor, at least partially, by way of the two relational facts mentioned above, qualified analysis endeavors to render the time effect as harmless as possible by trying to reduce it to spatial terms of juxtaposition and contiguity. The coexistent things are, as we have seen, arranged into the dimension of breadth, which we might accept provisionally. The fact of change is disposed of by imagining the single phases of the change to be arranged in the dimension of length as if the time during which these changes occurred were an extent in space along which the object moved. Obviously, the strange assumption is made that while the object "changes its place" along that stretch of time it also changes in some mysterious way its nature, that is, it undergoes the observed alterations of, say, aging.

In that way, sequence in time appears to bare and qualified analysis like a cinema in which a great number of single static pictures are substituted quickly enough to produce in the spectator the effect of moving figures. This illustration, after Bergson, is very frequently used in literature with or without the implication that, properly speaking, motion or change is illusory, or real to a lesser degree, while only the single static pictures, that is, self-identical physical and/or psychic (time) atoms, have genuine reality. But according to the Buddha the very reverse is true: change or flux is real, and the single static pictures (that is, individuals, atoms, etc.) are illusory.

If we take up another aspect of that same simile, we shall get a more correct view of the facts concerned: to take a film of moving objects with the help of a mechanism called a camera, and thereby to dissect the continuous motion of the objects, might be compared to the perceptual activity of the mind that, by necessity, must fictitiously arrest the flux of phenomena in order to discriminate. But, as in the case of the camera, that function of dissecting is only an artificial device based on the peculiarity of our perceptual instruments; it is not found in the actual phenomena any more than in the moving objects converted into static pictures by the camera. These static pictures obtained by filming correspond to the static images or percepts, concepts or notions, resulting from the act of perceiving.

But let us now leave this simile. We said before that the spatial world of qualified analysis is limited to the two dimensions of breadth and length. Bare or qualified analysis dare not admit those conditioning and conditioned phenomena that are bound up with the third dimension, that of depth, because the latter is too closely connected with the disturbing time factor. By "depth" we understand that subterranean flow of energies (a wide and intricate net of streams, rivers, and rivulets) originating in kamma or past actions and coming to the surface unexpectedly at a time determined by their inherent life rhythm (time required for growth, maturing, etc.) and by the influence of favorable or obstructive circumstances. The analytical method, we said, will admit only such relational energies as are transmitted by immediate impact (the dimension of breadth) or by the linear "wire" of immediate sequence (the dimension of length). But relational energies may also arise from unknown depths opening under the very feet of the individual or the object; or they may be transmitted, not by that linear "wire" of immediate sequence in space-time, but by way of "wireless" communication, traveling across vast distances in space and time. It is the time factor that gives depth and a wide and growing horizon to our worldview. By the time factor the "present moment" is freed from the banality and insignificance adhering to it in the equalizing and leveling world of space and one-sided analysis. The time factor, as emphasized by the philosophy of relations, invests the "present moment" with that dignity, significance, and decisive importance attributed to it by the Buddha and other great spiritual teachers. Only by the synthetical method, by the philosophy of relations, can due regard be given to the time factor, because in any comprehensive survey of relations or conditions, the past and future too have to be considered, while one-sided analysis may well neglect them.

Precisely because the following pages are mainly concerned with the analytical part of the Abhidhamma, we felt the need to underline the importance of the other aspect. But we wish to stress the harmonization of both methods, not only on philosophical grounds but also on account of its practical importance for spiritual development. Many will have observed in themselves or in others how greatly it often affects the entire life of the individual if the activity of mind is dominated by a dissecting (analytical) or connecting (synthetical) function, rather than the two being well balanced. The consequences can extend beyond the intellectual to the ethical, emotional, social, and imaginative side of the character. This can even be observed when one's own mental activity is temporarily engaged in one or the other direction. But it can be clearly seen in extreme analytical or synthetical types of mind; here the particular virtues and defects of both will be very marked. We need not enlarge on this. Enough has been said to point out how important it is for the formation of character, and for spiritual progress, to cultivate both the analytical and the synthetical faculties of one's mind. To do so is one aspect of following the Buddha's Middle Way, which alone leads to enlightenment.

III

The Schema of Classification in the *Dhammasaṅgaṇī*

The investigations undertaken in the following chapters are all based on the *first type of wholesome consciousness* dealt with in the first paragraph of the *Dhammasaṅgaṇī*. For the convenience of the reader a translation of it, preceded by the Pāli text, is given here. Each mental factor has been numbered to facilitate reference in the following pages; they will subsequently be referred to as F (= factor) 1, etc.

> Katame dhammā kusalā? Yasmiṁ samaye kāmāvacaraṁ kusalaṁ cittaṁ uppannaṁ hoti somanassa-sahagataṁ ñāṇa-sampayuttaṁ rūpārammaṇaṁ saddārammaṇaṁ gandhārammaṇaṁ, rasārammaṇaṁ phoṭṭhabbārammaṇaṁ dhammārammaṇaṁ, yaṁ yaṁ vā pan' ārabbha, tasmiṁ samaye phasso hoti vedanā hoti … avikkhepo hoti, ye vā pana tasmiṁ samaye aññe pi atthi paṭicca-samuppannā arūpino dhammā, ime dhammā kusalā.

> Which are the things that are wholesome? At a time when a state of wholesome consciousness belonging to the sensuous sphere has arisen accompanied by joy and associated with knowledge (and spontaneous), referring to any one object, be it an object of sight, sound, smell, taste, a tangible object, or a mental object—at that time there are present:

1. sense-contact (*phassa*) 2. feeling (*vedanā*) 3. perception (*saññā*) 4. volition (*cetanā*) 5. consciousness (*citta*)	The pentad of sense-contact (*phassa-pañcaka*)
6. thought (*vitakka*) 7. examination (*vicāra*) 8. rapture (*pīti*) 9. pleasure (*sukha*) 10. mental one-pointedness (*cittass'ekaggatā*)	Factors of absorption (*jhānaṅga*)
11. faculty of faith (*saddhindriya*) 12. " " energy (*viriyindriya*) 13. " " mindfulness (*satindriya*) 14. " " concentration (*samādhindriya*) 15. " " wisdom (*paññindriya*) 16. " " mind (*manindriya*) 17. " " joy (*somanassindriya*) 18. " " vitality (*jīvitindriya*)	Faculties (*indriya*)
19. right view (*sammā-diṭṭhi*) 20. " thought (*sammā-saṅkappa*) 21. " effort (*sammā-vāyāma*) 22. " mindfulness (*sammā-sati*) 23. " concentration (*sammā-samādhi*)	Path factors (*maggaṅga*)
24. power of faith (*saddhā-bala*) 25. " " energy (*viriya-bala*) 26. " " mindfulness (*sati-bala*) 27. " " concentration (*samādhi-bala*) 28. " " wisdom (*paññā-bala*) 29. " " moral shame (*hiri-bala*) 30. " " moral dread (*ottappa-bala*)	Powers (*bala*)

31. non-greed (*alobha*) 32. non-hatred (*adosa*) 33. non-delusion (*amoha*)	Wholesome roots (*kusala-mūla*)
34. non-covetousness (*anabhijjhā*) 35. non-ill will (*avyāpāda*) 36. right view (*sammā-diṭṭhi*)	Wholesome ways of action (*kusala-kammapatha*)
37. moral shame (*hiri*) 38. moral dread (*ottappa*)	The guardians of the world (*lokapāla*)
39. tranquillity of mental concomitants (*kāya-passaddhi*) 40. tranquillity of consciousness (*citta-passaddhi*) 41. agility of mental concomitants (*kāya-lahutā*) 42. agility of consciousness (*citta-lahutā*) 43. pliancy of mental concomitants (*kāya-mudutā*) 44. pliancy of consciousness (*citta-mudutā*) 45. workableness of mental concomitants (*kāya-kammaññatā*) 46. workableness of consciousness (*citta-kammaññatā*) 47. proficiency of mental concomitants (*kāya-pāguññatā*) 48. proficiency of consciousness (*citta-pāguññatā*) 49. uprightness of mental concomitants (*kāya-ujukatā*) 50. uprightness of consciousness (*citta-ujukatā*)	The six pairs (*yugalaka*)

51. mindfulness (*sati*) 52. mental clarity (*sampajañña*)	The helpers (*upakāraka*)
53. calm (*samatha*) 54. insight (*vipassanā*)	The paired combination (*yuganaddha*)
55. exertion (*paggāha*) 56. undistractedness (*avikkhepa*)	The last dyad (*piṭṭhi-dukā*)

These, or whatever other conditionally arisen incorporeal things there are at that time, these things are wholesome.

The "whatsoever other" (*ye-vā-panakā*), or supplementary factors, as given in the *Atthasālinī* are the following:

57. intention (*chanda*)
58. decision (*adhimokkha*)
59. attention (*manasikāra*)
60. mental equipoise (*tatramajjhattatā*)
61. compassion (*karuṇā*)
62. sympathetic joy (*muditā*)
63. abstinence from wrong bodily action (*kāyaduccarita-virati*)
64. abstinence from wrong speech (*vacīduccarita-virati*)
65. abstinence from wrong livelihood (*ājīvaduccarita-virati*)

The purpose of the first part of the *Dhammasaṅgaṇī*, the Consciousness Chapter (*cittuppādakaṇḍa*), is to give (1) a classification of all consciousness and (2) a detailed analysis of the single types of consciousness. The classification is given in the first clause of the principal sentences: "At a time when (such and such) a state of consciousness has arisen..." Here the respective type of consciousness is briefly characterized with the help of certain categories.

The detailed analysis follows in the concluding clause of the sentence: "...at that time there are: sense-contact," etc. This enumeration of mental factors will be called the "List of Dhammas." The word *dhamma*, of course, is here again used in the sense of thing or phenomenon.

The classifying categories used in the first part of the sentence refer to both the subjective and objective sides of the cognitive process.

1. The statements about the "subject" concern:

a. the plane or sphere of consciousness (*bhūmi*), in our example: the sensuous sphere

b. the kammic value, here: wholesome

c. the emotional value, here: joyful

d. presence or absence of knowledge, here: associated with knowledge

e. spontaneous or nonspontaneous occurrence, here: spontaneous

2. The statement about the "object" is generally not used for constituting separate classes of consciousness. The six kinds of sense objects are considered only as variations of the same type. In nearly all cases it is the "subjective" relation to the object which is used for the differentiation of consciousness. The objects determine the classification only in the case of the five types of sense consciousness: eye-consciousness…body-consciousness. These belong to the most primitive phase of the perceptual process, immediately following the first "adverting of the mind" (*āvajjana*), when the impact of the object is predominant. In this phase the activity of the subjective factors is still weak, as shown by the small number of mental concomitants present in these types of consciousness.

From the above subjective categories *a–e*, the following are anticipations of factors contained in the complete analysis as given in the List of Dhammas:

b. The kammic value, here "wholesome," is determined by the presence of the "wholesome roots." If the state of consciousness is "associated with knowledge," as in our case, all three roots are present, namely, non-greed, non-hate, and non-delusion (F31, 32, 33); if "dissociated from knowledge," non-delusion (= knowledge) is missing.

c. The emotional value, here "joyful," is represented by the factors: feeling (F2), pleasure (F9), and joy (F17).

d. The association with, and dissociation from, knowledge is determined by the presence or absence of the third wholesome root, non-delusion (F33), and its various synonyms or aspects (e.g., F15, 19, etc.).

The category of spontaneous or nonspontaneous occurrence cannot be traced to any factor of the respective present moment of consciousness but depends on previous mental processes. We speak of "spontaneous" if the reaction or decision takes place without being prompted, by force of inclination or habit, both of which may have their roots in a distant past or even in a previous existence. We speak of "nonspontaneous" if the reaction or decision is preceded by one's own deliberation or by an outer influence in the way of advice, request, or command; so the nonspontaneity of a state of consciousness may be due either to premeditation or to instigation.

IV

The List of Mental Constituents in the *Dhammasaṅgaṇī*

In psychology a difference of aspects is a difference in things.
—James Ward, "Psychology," *Ency. Brit.*, 9th ed.

1. General Remarks

When one reads through the List of Dhammas as given in the *Dhammasaṅgaṇī*, this list appears, at first sight, to heap up rather arbitrarily and superfluously a great number of synonyms, thus presenting a strange contrast to the otherwise terse, lucid, and strictly systematic plan of that work. Precisely this striking contrast will make us hesitate to ascribe the seemingly unsystematic character of the list to a lack of the most elementary skill in methodical exposition. If we look at the admirable architecture of the *Dhammasaṅgaṇī's* ground plan and details, we shall certainly not be willing to suppose that its author—be it the Buddha himself or his early disciples—was incapable of neatly summarizing parallel factors under a single heading, as was done in such later works as the *Atthasālinī*, the *Visuddhimagga*, and the *Abhidhammattha-saṅgaha*.

The *Atthasālinī* actually discusses a criticism alleging lack of system and superfluity of repetitions in the List of Dhammas. The commentator puts into the mouth of the critic the following drastic indictment: "It is a disconnected exposition, as disorderly as booty carried off by thieves or grass scattered by a herd of cattle in their track. It is made without any understanding of the matter"

(*Asl* 135). The commentator meets that criticism with the following simile: A king levies a tax on the different crafts and professions, commanding that those who execute several crafts pay the corresponding amount of tax units. Now, the different professional activities of a single person correspond to the different functions of a single factor of consciousness. The number of tax units payable by the same person are to be compared to the number of classifications corresponding to the various functions of a single factor.

This simile, however, only explains the inclusion of parallel factors, regarded separately and as functions of a single mental quality. It does not do justice to another important fact that properly rounds off and completes the explanations, namely, the arrangement of these quasi-synonyms into groups. A factor, by force of its various functions, enters into combination with various sets of other factors grouped around a common function or purpose. This fact is important because these very groups represent the formal principle of arrangement in our list. The names of these groups (as given on pp. 32–34) are assigned to them partly in the text of the *Dhammasaṅgaṇī* itself in the *Saṅgahavāra,* i.e., Summary Section, and partly in the *Atthasālinī,* but the fact of the grouping is quite evident from the list itself. On the other hand, if the grouping were nothing more than a formal principle of arrangement, it would not have been allowed to determine the composition of the list. Though the predilection of the Indian mind for purely formalistic methods of exposition is well known, this peculiarity rarely impairs the treatment of the subject matter itself. And it would certainly not be permitted to do so in this case, in a work that offers psychological instruction in a form so tersely concentrated and reduced to the bare essentials with no embellishments. We cannot suppose that in a work of this character the List of Dhammas should have been cluttered with tautologies merely for formalistic reasons. The groups among which we find these different parallel terms are more than devices of arrangement; they are also psychic realities in themselves, for they represent purposive associations of single factors, that is, their concurrent directions of movement and their common tendencies of development. We shall soon give an example for a single factor's membership in several groups and shall deal with it further in the chapters that follow, which are devoted to the various groups.

The introduction of partly overlapping groups indicates the subtle and complicated structure of a moment of consciousness. It shows that a psychic unit is not "composed" of rigid parts, arranged, as it were, in juxtaposition like a mosaic, but is rather a relational and correlational system of dynamic processes.

In order to give to the groups the place they deserve within the simile of the *Atthasālinī* quoted above, we may supplement it by adding that the person executing various professions and paying the corresponding taxes should also belong to each of the respective professional guilds, which would correspond to the groupings. But the different applications of one faculty may become clearer by another simile, and if the simile chosen by the teachers of old is somewhat banal, that will be an excuse if ours is likewise so.

Let us suppose a man, as the head of his family, is in charge of the household purse; in his professional capacity he is a cashier, and in his club its treasurer. Thus his general skill in reckoning is applied to different aspects of life and to the different social groups to which he belongs. Consequently his skill serves different purposes, to attain which he has to combine it, in each case, with some quite different qualities of his own. It also brings him into contact with quite different sorts of people. The application to our case is this: Our man's general skill in reckoning corresponds to a single factor (viewed in the abstract) belonging to a certain moment of consciousness. The three practical applications of that skill are the different actual functions of that factor. The various other faculties that our man has to summon to his aid in the three different spheres of his activity correspond to the other members of those groups to which our factor belongs; they signify the *internal* relations within the same moment of consciousness. The fact that the man is executing his skill in different kinds of environment, and meets there different sorts of people, corresponds to the *external* relations to other states of consciousness, which may belong to the same or a different classificatory type.

The various functions of a mental factor might start quite different lines of development, that is, enter into different external relations. For example, one-pointedness of mind (*cittass'ekaggatā*) can be deliberately cultivated as a factor of meditative absorption (*jhānaṅga*) and be developed up to the degree of complete absorption of mind (*appanā*). Or with emphasis on its liberating quality, one-pointedness may have the aspect of the path factor of right concentration, and it can be developed for the purpose of insight (*vipassanā*) only up to access concentration (*upacāra-samādhi*). Or one-pointedness may appear as calm (*samatha*) in the paired combination of calm and insight (F53, 54).

At first it will be a single function or aspect of a mental factor that initiates a certain external relation with the succeeding moments of consciousness, but this does not exclude other aspects of the same factor also manifesting themselves more prominently in later states of consciousness. In the same way the relative strength or weakness of any factor might have no visible consequence just now but may produce effects at some later moment when conditions are favorable. The net of relations, conditions, or causes extending from a single moment of consciousness may reach very far in space as well as in time.

The relational system of the functions within a single moment of consciousness extends not only to the future but also to the multiplicity of past states of consciousness that are its conditions. That is to say: mental factors, far from being self-contained units, are "open" toward the past as well as the future, and, though meeting in one moment, they are related to quite different "layers" of those time periods. From that we can gauge the highly dynamic nature of the processes going on in a single moment of consciousness.

All these facts, and other reasons too, exclude the assumption of later Buddhist schools, for example, the Sarvāstivādins, that the *dhammas* or mental factors are a kind of Platonic ideas or psychic atoms in the literal sense of being indivisible. These schools have misunderstood the old grammarian's definition of *dhamma* (Skt *dharma*)—*attano sabhāvaṁ dhārenti*—as implying that each *dhamma* is the "bearer" of a single quality (*sabhāva*) or of a single characteristic (*lakkhaṇa*). But, in the true spirit of Buddhist philosophy, that definition means only that the *dhammas* are not reducible by further retrogression to any substantial bearers of qualities. It does not imply that these *dhammas* themselves are such "substances" or "bearers," nor are they to be distinguished in any way from their qualities or functions, which in no phase of their existence can be said to have self-identity. The *Mūlaṭīkā* (the subcommentary to the *Dhammasaṅgaṇī*) says (p. 28): "There is no other thing than the quality borne by it" (na ca dhāriyamāna-sabhāvā añño dhammo nāma atthi). And these things (*dhammā*) themselves, as the *Atthasālinī* expressly says (p. 39), "are borne by their conditions" (*paccayehi dharīyanti*). Therefore they cannot be said to be ultimate, that is, unconditioned "bearers." Furthermore, it is impossible to speak of a thing as the bearer of a single quality in a strict sense, if the functions of the respective factor, its direction of movement, its intensity, and its kammic quality are variable, in accordance with the relational system to which that factor belongs.

Now here are a few illustrations of possible variations of so-called "identical" factors or qualities. We have already mentioned the varying functions, directions of movement, and degrees of intensity in the case of mental one-pointedness (p. 40), and we add what follows. The intensity of one-pointedness may sink to such a low level that this fact is expressly registered in the *Dhammasaṅgaṇī* by an abbreviation of the stereotype definition, restricting it to mere "stability" (*ṭhiti*); the terms denoting greater intensity (*saṇṭhiti, avaṭṭhiti,* etc.) are left out. Variations with regard to kammic quality are shown, for example, by the fact that one-pointedness is present in unwholesome consciousness too. Even such an elementary factor as perception (*saññā*) is not unequivocal. According to the *Atthasālinī* and the *Mūlaṭīkā*, its reliability and steadfastness are dependent on the presence or absence of knowledge and on a higher or lower degree of concentration.

Furthermore, even consecutive states of consciousness of the same type, having the same mental factors, are not strictly identical. The very fact that they are conditioned by repetition (*āsevanā-paccaya*) means that certain factors are intensified by force of practice. But even this effect of repetition or habit is not stationary in any phase. After gradually reaching its peak, the effect will wear off, and certain factors, for example, interest (*pīti*) will become weak. There is yet another reason why the first occurrence of a state of consciousness differs from its repetition: at the first occurrence an outer stimulus may have been the primary condition (e.g., by way of decisive support condition, *upanissaya-paccaya*), while for the repetition the primary condition will be the previous occurrence of the corresponding state of consciousness itself—a circumstance that will certainly give a different character to the subsequent repetition.

In view of such numerous possible variations even among so-called identical factors of the same type of consciousness, there is no justification for believing in any unchangeable "bearers" of definite qualities.

By arranging the mental factors in relational groups a subordinate synthetical element has been introduced into the mainly analytical *Dhammasaṅgaṇī*. By so doing, the danger inherent in purely analytical methods has been avoided. This danger consists in erroneously taking for genuine separate entities the "parts" resulting from analysis, instead of restricting their use to sound practical method with the purpose of classifying and dissolving composite events wrongly conceived as ultimate unities. It has been a regular occurrence in the history of physics, metaphysics, and psychology that when a "whole" has been successfully dissolved by analysis, the resultant "parts" themselves come in turn to be regarded as little "wholes." Early Buddhist schools succumbed to this danger, for example, the Vaibhāshika or Sarvāstivāda, which belongs to the so-called Hīnayāna. It was these schools that defined *dhammas* as "substantial bearers of their specific exclusive qualities."[23] They assumed that "the *substance* of all things has a permanent existence throughout the three divisions of time, present, past, and future"[24] and that only the manifestations of these "substantial bearers" were impermanent and subject to change in the three divisions of time. The teachings of these schools were probably the reason why "Hīnayāna" in general has been called a "pluralistic" doctrine by Mahāyāna thinkers as well as by some modern scholars.[25] But this statement is certainly not applicable to the Theravāda school and still less to the Pāli Canon itself, as is amply proved in these pages. Besides, the charge of "pluralism" cannot be restricted to Hīnayāna alone, since quite a number of Mahāyāna schools too accepted this pluralistic "*dharma* theory," as Rosenberg has shown.

On the other hand, a prominent Mahāyāna school—the Mādhyamikas—vigorously rejected and criticized the pluralistic *dharma* theory. In relation to what we said about the "twofold method of the Abhidhamma," it is significant that this criticism of pluralism comes from the Mādhyamikas, a school that particularly emphasized the synthetical method, that is, the philosophy of relations, against one-sided analysis that too easily tends to become dogmatic. The Mādhyamikas even exaggerated the application of that principle by denying the ultimate validity of the formula of dependent origination and of the modes of conditionality. By doing so, they carried the principle of relativity to an extreme where it destroys its own basis. However, by rejecting the other extreme, that of one-sided analysis, this Mahāyāna school has preserved the spirit of the pure doctrine, at least in this respect, more faithfully than the Hīnayāna school of the Sarvāstivādins. We should emphasize once more that in our opinion the genuine tradition of the Theravāda is not affected by that criticism, provided that its standpoint is formulated with due caution, that is, by using both the analytical and the synthetical method, as the Buddha has done in the suttas as well as in the Abhidhamma. By following the Master's example, the danger of converting or perverting concepts of relative validity into entities of ultimate reality will be avoided.

From the mistaken assumption of separate units of whatever description—ultimate *dharmas*, Platonic ideas, atoms, elements, qualities, traits of character, etc.—follows the belief in the actual existence of some kind of clear-cut opposites. In this context we shall say a few words about one pair of opposites only: identity and diversity. These opposites have no absolute validity but are relative terms denoting various degrees of similitude or divergence indicating different grades in the closeness and range of ever-present relations. The ultimate reality of these two terms has been denied by many philosophical systems, but this denial has a truly secure foundation only in a doctrine that disposes of substantiality as radically as thc Buddhist philosophy of relations does. We would emphasize again that "voidness of substance," the *anattā* doctrine, can be established securely only with the aid of an all-comprehensive philosophy of relations, and not by analysis alone.

The Buddhist philosophy of relations shows that there is no complete identity or diversity in life, but only a continuous process of identifying or diversifying, of assimilating and dissimilating. A persistent struggle goes on between these two forces, resulting in merely a temporary dominance of one but never in the complete exclusion of the other. In every phase of assimilation there is an irreducible remainder of diversity making for dissimilation; and in every phase of dissimilation there is an irreducible remainder of identity making for assimilation.

These factors also furnish the explanation of the famous Buddhist dictum on the problem of rebirth: "it is neither the same nor another" who is reborn.[26] The differences in each and every mental and corporeal factor forming the two concatenations involved in the process of rebirth exclude "sameness," that is, the ego-identity of a transmigrating soul. But the existing close relations between these two series of life processes exclude absolute diversity between the "old" and the "new" existences. These close relations are represented, for example, by the correspondence between the rebirth-producing kamma and the resultant rebirth-consciousness, and by the immediate contiguity of death-consciousness (*cuti-citta*) and rebirth-consciousness (*paṭisandhi-citta*). The same principle—"neither the same nor another"—holds true also for normal consciousness during life: for though there is no identity between successive states of consciousness, there is also no complete diversity since some factors and groups always overlap. In our analogy of the man with three different fields of activity, the relative identity is represented by his general skill in reckoning, which forms the common basis for all three of his activities. The relative diversity is shown by the application of that skill in different social spheres (i.e., difference of groupings), in a different manner (i.e., difference of functions), and with different purposes (i.e., difference in the direction of movement).

To express it generally: Absolute *identity* is excluded by the internal differentiation of things, that is, by the differences of intensity, function, direction, and composition existing in even apparently identical phenomena. Absolute *diversity* is excluded by the continuity and interdependence of things, which restrict the effects of the differentiating tendencies.

Contemplating the relativity of these two concepts, identity and diversity, will make clear the true nature of change or impermanence (*aniccatā*). It will show that change always involves two complementary aspects, dissolution and connection, which are like two faces turned in opposite directions. The fact of change implies both the breaking off of old connections and the establishing of new ones. Change performs simultaneously a twofold function: dissimilating or diversifying, and assimilating or identifying. When expounding the characteristic of impermanence, the suttas and also popular treatises on Buddhism stress that aspect of change that consists in separation, dissolution, or dissimilation. This particular emphasis is fully justified insofar as the ultimate purpose of Buddhist instruction is a practical one, final deliverance of the mind, which can be reached only when the last traces of belief in (*diṭṭhi*) and craving for (*taṇhā*) an ego-identity or any other kind of substantiality are destroyed. The negative aspect of change, the final separation and dissolution inherent in all composite things, furnishes the strongest emotional call to the practical renunciation needed to strive for the goal of liberation. At least this will be so with most people, though not with all; for there are some who firmly believe (or pretend) that they enjoy "variety" for its own sake, at any cost.

Theoretical or philosophical understanding of reality, too, must start with the dissimilating aspect of change, that is, with its dissolving effect on apparently ultimate units. This corresponds to the precedence that analysis takes in Buddhist philosophy in general as well as in the practice of meditation. The first task of insight (*vipassanā*) is what the commentators call *ghanavinibbhoga*, the dissecting of an apparently compact mass. This might have been the reason why, in arranging the seven books of the Abhidhamma, the first place has been given to the analytical *Dhammasaṅgaṇī* and the last place to the synthetical *Paṭṭhāna*. Both books are equal in importance, but in the method of procedure analysis comes first. Nevertheless, while acknowledging the great practical and theoretical importance of contemplating the dissolving aspect of change, we must also give due attention to its connecting function. Only by doing so will a well-balanced view of reality be obtained, which is indispensable for endowing insight with its full liberating power.

The apparent repetitions in the List of Dhammas demonstrate (1) the multiple internal relations that obtain among the factors within a single moment of consciousness and (2) the multiple external relations that any moment of consciousness and its factors has with past and future moments. This twofold plurality of relations has its parallel in the twofold "differentiation" (*cittatā*) of consciousness that the *Atthasālinī* mentions in its didactic definition of *citta*: (1) consciousness *is differentiated in itself* with regard to its object, its sphere (*bhūmi*), its quality, etc.; (2) it *produces differentiation* (*cittakaraṇa*) by causing various activities in the outer world, and in the case of kammic consciousness by producing various rebirth processes.[27]

The microscope and the subtle experimental methods of modern science have analyzed and "smashed" ever smaller material units until the most minute results are no more directly perceptible but only deducible from observed phenomena. Modern research has penetrated to a point where even the least accessible components of the material world have lost their static appearance and have been recognized as dynamic processes. What is here the gradual result of painstaking research through many hundreds of years, by many hundreds of scientists, was achieved with regard to the "psychic atom" by a single great thinker—the Buddha. With a unique power of penetration in which intuition of genius was combined with scientific method, the master mind of the Buddha showed by analysis that even the smallest—and likewise only deducible—psychic unit is not uniform and homogeneous but varied and complex; and in his complementary philosophy of relations he showed that this complexity is not static but dynamic.

In the detailed treatment of the single groups of mental constituents that follows, the opinion is expressed that, at least in parts, an intentional order exists in their sequence. Such opinion seems to be expressly rejected in the following passage of the *Atthasālinī* (p. 107):

> Concerning the mental factors arising in a single moment of consciousness, it is not possible to say that one appears first

> and another later.... Sense-contact is mentioned first only by reason of sequence in the exposition. One could as well enumerate them as follows: "There is feeling, sense-contact..."; or, "There is feeling, perception, thinking, etc." Just as here so in the case of the other factors too, one should not inquire into the sequence of what comes earlier and later.

This objection does not invalidate our opinion that the groups of factors in the list are enumerated in an intentional order. Obviously, the commentarial objection is directed only against the supposition that the arrangement of the list implies a sequence in time. This, of course, is not the case, for the simple reason that all these factors appear simultaneously in a single moment of consciousness. But the assumption that the list gives, for the purpose of exposition, a meaningful and not arbitrary sequence is not contradicted by that objection. We maintain only that there is an interconnection between certain *factors,* as established already by the fact of grouping, and that there is also an interrelation among some of these *groups.* Further, we believe that, at least in some cases, the particular character of the groups explains why some are enumerated before others. The commentary is surely carried away by its argument if, in the passage quoted above, it intends to imply that the arrangement of the single factors is purely arbitrary. In the last example of possible variations given by the *Atthasālinī* in the passage quoted above, even members of different groups have been mixed together. Against that it should be remembered that the canonical text itself emphasizes the fact and the importance of the group arrangement by regularly adding a Summary Section (*saṅgahavāra*) that serves to indicate which groups and how many group members are present in the particular type of consciousness.

We have to admit, however, that only in the case of the first six or eight groups have we been able to establish an interconnection. But even if it should not be possible to find any such connection between the other groups, this would not exclude an inner relation among the first groups, which contain the most important concrete factors on their first occurrence in the list. In any case our observations on that point may contribute to the achievement of a better understanding of the distinctive characteristics of the groups and of the manner in which they operate within a single moment of consciousness: in other words, a better comprehension of the complicated inner relations prevailing in a conscious moment.

In these "General Remarks" not all reasons have been mentioned that may be assumed to have motivated the inclusion of parallel factors in the list. Additional reasons will result from the detailed survey of the single groups that follows and a summary will be given in the "Concluding Remarks."

2. The Pentad of Sense-Contact *(phassa-pañcaka, F1–5)*

The first five factors enumerated in the list are called, in the *Atthasālinī*, *phassa-pañcaka*, "the pentad (beginning) with sense-contact." These five are the basic non-rational elements in every state of consciousness and therefore rightly claim the first place in the list. They are also the briefest formulation, by way of representatives, of the four mental aggregates (*khandha*). The aggregates of feeling and perception are represented by the same terms (F2, F3); for the aggregate of consciousness (*viññāṇakkhandha*) the synonymous term *citta* (F5) is given; the aggregate of mental formations (*saṅkhārakkhandha*) is represented by two of its most typical general factors, sense-contact (F1) and volition (F4).[28]

A fundamental axiom of Buddhist psychology finds expression in the composition of that pentad: the inseparableness of the four mental aggregates, namely, feeling, perception, mental formations, and consciousness. Even in the weakest state of consciousness (including subconsciousness) all of them are represented.

Verification of the Terms in the Suttas

In order to illustrate how widely the Abhidhamma is based on the Sutta Piṭaka we shall now trace the respective Abhidhamma terms to their source in the suttas. We shall do so in the following sections, too, but only where it is not evident and of particular interest.

The name of the pentad occurs as *phassa-pañcamā* in the *Theragāthā* in a verse (v. 907) spoken by the Elder Anuruddha on the occasion of the Buddha's passing away: ete pacchimakā dāni munino phassa-pañcamā, "these are now the last pentads of sense-contact of the Sage." This seems to be the only sutta passage where the group's name appears. But the five terms constituting the group are frequently mentioned seriatim. They appear, for example, in a longer sequence of doctrinal terms in the *Mahā Satipaṭṭhāna Sutta* (*DN* II 308–9) and at the beginning of the *Rāhula-saṁyutta*: "visual consciousness... visual contact... feeling produced by visual contact... perception of visual objects... volition relating to visual objects..."[29] Here the order of enumeration and the names of the factors differs slightly from that in the *Dhammasaṅgaṇī*, but all the five are consecutively given.

These terms occur also in the *Anupada Sutta* (*MN* No. 111), a text that is of particular interest for a study of the genesis of the Abhidhamma. There the five factors are mentioned among others as the result of a psychological analysis of meditative consciousness, undertaken in retrospect by the Venerable Sāriputta after rising from jhāna, meditative absorption. The passage referring to the first absorption reads as follows: "The things occurring in the first jhāna, namely, thought, examination, rapture, pleasure, and mental one-pointedness; *sense-contact, feeling, perception, volition, consciousness,* intention, decision, energy, mindfulness, equanimity, attention—these things (or mental factors) were determined by him one after the other."[30] Here the five factors of absorption (*jhānaṅga*) are enumerated first, being the main characteristics of jhānic consciousness to which that retrospective analysis refers. Then our pentad of sense-contact follows, with its members named in the same order as in the *Dhammasaṅgaṇī*.

In this sutta the Buddha calls this mode of analysis *anupada-dhamma-vipassanā*, i.e., "insight into things taken one after the other," and he states further that the Venerable Sāriputta practiced it for a fortnight prior to his attainment of arahantship. During that period, "these things were determined by him one after another," which the commentary explains as meaning that the nature of these mental factors was defined by him through their characteristics (*lakkhaṇa*). The analysis given in the discourse extends to all nine absorptions and represents a precursor of the detailed analysis of meditative consciousness found in the *Dhammasaṅgaṇī*. So we may regard this fortnight of Sāriputta's practice of analytical insight as one of the germ cells of the later Abhidhamma literature. The *Anupada Sutta* shows that an elaboration of the doctrine in the manner of the Abhidhamma had already been undertaken in the Master's lifetime by analytically and philosophically gifted disciples. This development was expressly encouraged by the Buddha when, in that discourse, he praised Sāriputta's fortnight of analytical inquiry.

Also two traditional views expressed, for example, in the *Atthasālinī*, are supported by the *Anupada Sutta.*

1. One is the Venerable Sāriputta's close connection with the origin and the handing down of the Abhidhamma. According to an ancient Buddhist tradition Sāriputta was the first human being to whom the Buddha taught the Abhidhamma after he had expounded it in the Tāvatiṁsa heaven.[31]

2. It tallies also with the statement (at *Asl* 16) that Sāriputta had only elaborated upon the "method" (*naya*) or key terms of the Abhidhamma, which had been indicated to him by the Buddha, the progenitor of the system. With regard to the pentad of sense-contact, Sāriputta may well have taken as such an indication the terms of the *Mahā Satipaṭṭhāna Sutta* mentioned above, and made use of them in his psychological analysis of jhānic consciousness.[32]

As to the origin of the Abhidhamma, we are inclined to think that the Buddha did not regard it as his task to expound his Abhidhammic knowledge in full detail, but in his pedagogical career he was primarily moved by the wish to give the first decisive spiritual impulse and instruction to as many beings as possible. Instead of giving difficult and detailed philosophical expositions comprehensible only to a few, the Buddha mostly preferred to repeat, all the more frequently, the fundamental features of his liberating doctrine bearing the distinct stamp of his first great inspiration under the Bodhi Tree. This is impressively demonstrated by the very numerous repetitions or slight variations of those fundamental expositions faithfully recorded in the Sutta Piṭaka by the monks of old. A striking example of these repetitions or variations is the last book of the Saṁyutta Nikāya, the *Mahāvagga*.

In accordance with his frequent appeal to the listener's own effort and judgment, the Buddha usually left it to his followers to develop for themselves the spiritual or intellectual impulse imparted by him and to apply it to their personal practice and understanding. In particular he left it to those of his disciples who were especially proficient in certain theoretical or practical areas to give additional help and instruction to those in need of it. This is clearly shown by the often recurring passages in the suttas where monks ask the Buddha for a brief summary of the Dhamma or a terse maxim for use as their subject of meditation. Sometimes we read that these monks later approached one of the chief disciples and asked for an elucidation. So it is quite probable that the Buddha transmitted the gist of his Abhidhammic knowledge to such individual monks as he knew would be capable of elaborating and applying the briefly indicated summary by their own penetrative intellect, as for example the Venerable Sāriputta. This hypothesis of ours agrees with the commentarial statement that the Buddha transmitted to Sāriputta only the *mātikā*, the matrix of the Abhidhamma. From this we may also conclude that the ancient tradition regarded the Buddha as the *auctor* but not the author of the Abhidhamma books, that is, as the creative genius to whom the ideas and perhaps the frame of the system, but not the literary formulation, should be ascribed.

The Pentad in the Post-canonical Pāli Literature

Apart from the single reference to the name of the pentad we were able to trace in the *Theragāthā* of the Sutta Piṭaka, the group's name appears only in the post-canonical period, first probably in the *Nettippakaraṇa*, in the variant *phassa-pañcamaka*.[33] We have to assume this work to be earlier than (or at least contemporary with) Buddhaghosa, as the latter quotes it under the abbreviated name "the treatise" (*pakaraṇa*) in his commentary to the *Satipaṭṭhāna Sutta*. But it is possible that the term *phassa-pañcaka* was already in the old commentaries on which Buddhaghosa's works were based. This seems more probable than the assumption that the term was first coined in the *Nettippakaraṇa.*

The relevant passage runs as follows: "Mentality-materiality" (*nāma-rūpa*) are the five aggregates forming the objects of grasping. Here, the things having sense-contact as their fifth (*phassa-pañcamakā dhammā*) are "mentality" (*nāma*). The five physical sense faculties are "materiality" (*rūpa*). Both together are "mentality-materiality" connected with consciousness (*viññāṇa-sampayuttaṁ*).[34]

From the separate mention of *viññāṇa* in the last sentence, we have to conclude that in this passage "consciousness" (*viññāṇa* or *citta*) is not included in the pentad. Probably *manasikāra* ("attention") takes its place, being mentioned in another passage of the *Nettippakaraṇa* (p. 78) where six factors are enumerated, including *citta*: "Feeling, perception, volition, consciousness, sense-contact, attention—these are called the mental group (*nāmakāya*)." The enumeration in this passage is derived from the *Sammādiṭṭhi Sutta* (*MN* I 53).

Buddhaghosa (at least according to the manuscripts and editions available today) uses both forms of the term. For example, in his commentary on the *Satipaṭṭhāna Sutta* we find *phassa-pañcaka* in the section on mindfulness of breathing, and *phassa-pañcamaka* in the section on the contemplation of feeling.[35] There the five components of the pentad are identical with those in the *Dhammasaṅgaṇī*, that is, including *citta* and excluding *manasikāra.*

Before Buddhaghosa's time the same five factors occur in the *Milindapañha*, in the same order, but without the group name (p. 87). But in this work there is also a passage (p. 59) where, in giving a representative selection of mental concomitants, *manasikāra* too is included: "And the Elder enlightened King Milinda with words from the Abhidhamma: 'The origin of visual consciousness, O King, is dependent on the sense organ of sight and visual objects. And such things as arise simultaneously, namely, sense-contact, feeling, perception, volition, concentration, vitality, and attention, arise in dependence thereon.'" It is worth pointing out that this enumeration agrees with the seven general mental factors (*sabbacittasādhāraṇa cetasika*) mentioned in the later Abhidhamma works.[36] It is significant that Buddhaghosa does not mention this group of seven factors in his *Atthasālinī*. His reason for not doing so was most probably the fact that the lists in the *Dhammasaṅgaṇī* commented upon in the *Atthasālinī* are not meant to give an abstract and systematic arrangement of factors but refer to definite moments of consciousness in their dynamic actuality, where these factors appear as members of relational groups.

To the difference consisting in inclusion and exclusion of *manasikāra* we shall revert when dealing with the supplementary factors (§14 below).

3. The Factors of Absorption *(jhānaṅga, F6–10)*

The group of five factors that follows now is well known through its frequent occurrence in the suttas to represent the most characteristic constituents of the first jhāna (see p. 49). Their group name, "factors of absorption" (*jhānaṅga*), does not occur in the suttas.[37] But we find it in the *Dhammasaṅgaṇī* where it occurs, rather unexpectedly, in the Summary Section relating to the first class of wholesome consciousness (*Dhs* §§58, 83). This state of consciousness, the subject of our present analysis, does not belong to jhānic consciousness of the sphere of form (*rūpāvacara*) but to normal consciousness of the sensuous sphere (*kāmāvacara*). Evidently the term "jhāna" is used in this compound in a wider application to refer to any stronger "absorption" in an object, any intensive concentration on it, whether in a meditative attainment or otherwise. The term is also used in this wider sense in the expression *jhāna-paccaya*, "condition by way of absorption," one of the twenty-four modes of conditionality belonging to the framework of the *Paṭṭhāna*. This condition is exercised not only by meditative states of mind, that is, by jhāna proper, but by nearly all the more active types of consciousness in all spheres (*bhūmi* or *avacara*). Each of the five "factors of absorption" functions as such a condition because it exercises an intensifying influence both on the other associated good or bad mental factors arising in the same unit of consciousness as well as on the simultaneously arisen corporeal phenomena. Even more than that: not only do they influence corporeal phenomena, but according to commentarial tradition it is their presence that enables a state of consciousness to produce corporeal phenomena.[38]

Now, on the basis of the above discussion, we can express more distinctly the general function of the *jhānaṅgas* in their wider sense by denoting them as *intensifying factors.* In doing so, we are supported by the *Mūlaṭīkā* to the *Khandha-vibhaṅga*, where they are spoken of as *bala-dāyakā*, "strength-givers."[39]

We shall now briefly examine the single factors composing this group. *Pleasure* or happiness (*sukha*, F9) was already included, under the name "feeling" (*vedanā*, F2), in the pentad of sense-contact. But since pleasant feeling may have a strongly intensifying effect on the respective state of consciousness and contribute to the absorption in the object, it also enters into the factors of absorption. Here we meet the first multiple classification of factors and overlapping of groups. In the case of the type of consciousness treated here, "feeling" in the pentad corresponds to "pleasure" among the factors of absorption. In other classes of consciousness feeling may correspond to pain (*dukkha*) or to indifference (*upekkhā*). The fact that (mental) pain, too, counts as a factor of absorption illustrates the extended meaning in which the term *jhānaṅga* is used here.

Compared with the relatively primitive and non-rational (we may even say pre-rational) character of the pentad of sense-contact, where the grasp of the object is still weak and incomplete, the factors of absorption represent a phase of consciousness where a rational element has entered and which at the same time possesses a higher degree of *differentiation* and *intensity.* The rational factors are *thought* (*vitakka*, F6) and *examination* (*vicāra*, F7). It is these two that are primarily responsible for the greater *differentiation* and complexity of consciousness, and also for its greater agility, while all five factors serve to *intensify* the activity of consciousness in general.

The intensifying effect of *pīti* (F8) in its two aspects of *rapture* and *interest* is a quite evident fact. But above all *mental one-pointedness* or *concentration* (*cittass'ekaggatā,* F10) is the main force making for intensification and absorption, which it does by counteracting any distracting influences. A minimal degree of concentration is indispensable in every state of consciousness, even the weakest, in order to enable it to interrupt the stream of subconsciousness (*bhavaṅga*), and therefore mental one-pointedness belongs to the seven mental concomitants common to all consciousness.[40] But it is only in the more active classes of consciousness that it is counted as a factor of absorption.

Now one may ask why one-pointedness, being such a fundamental factor, was not added to the first group of the list, the pentad. In reply we suggest that it was included among the factors of absorption, first, because it is the most typical factor of jhāna consciousness and is so often enumerated among the jhāna factors in the suttas, while, as we have seen, the pentad forms a distinct unit in the older sources, too. Second, mental one-pointedness or concentration is the general factor that plays the most decisive role in the further development of consciousness, and therefore its rightful place is among the intensifying factors of absorption. Still, one may ask why it was not included in both groups, the pentad and the factors of absorption, all the more so since mental one-pointedness does appear in our list under a great number of headings anyway. The answer is that the *Dhammasaṅgaṇī* is not concerned with the formal or abstract arrangement of factors, for example, whether they are common to all consciousness, but only with the actual function of a factor within a given state of consciousness and within the group of factors. These groups are more than a formal principle of arrangement; they register the common denominator or purpose of the various single factors or functions. In that strict sense the pentad does not form a homogeneous group, and perhaps for that reason it is not mentioned as such in the Summary Section of the *Dhammasaṅgaṇī*, but the factors constituting it are enumerated there singly: "There is one sense-contact, one feeling, etc." The group name *phassa-pañcaka* is found only in the *Atthasālinī*, having been taken from other sources as mentioned above.

It is worth noting that the intensifying factors of absorption follow immediately after the relatively primitive pentad of sense-contact, which is fully developed in the dullest consciousness, even in that of animals. This juxtaposition of a relatively low level of mind with one possessing vast potentialities points to the thought-provoking fact that from an average state of consciousness movement in two opposite directions is possible. The downward way resulting from an insufficient cultivation of the intensifying factors leads to a gradual weakening, dulling, and animal-like degeneration of consciousness, which in due time may even end in an actual rebirth as an animal. The upward way is the development and strengthening of the factors of absorption. In its progress this development may quite transcend the coarse and crude consciousness of the sensual sphere (*kāmāvacara*), which limits the intensification of consciousness, and may rise to a different plane of mind: to the meditative or jhānic consciousness of the sphere of form (*rūpāvacara*), incomparably more intense, powerful, luminous, and agile. This ascent to a higher level may be of brief duration in one who attains the meditative absorptions during life in the world of sense; or it may be of longer duration through rebirth into the world of form (*rūpaloka*), where this refined state of mind is the normal condition of consciousness.

This shows that the seeds of "another world," i.e., of a higher level of consciousness, are present in the average human mind, where they are waiting to be nursed to full growth and fruition. It shows that these two worlds are not separated from each other by an abyss to be overcome only by a forcible leap or by "divine grace." The two worlds, the sensuous and the jhānic, meet and overlap within our everyday consciousness. From the figurative expression "seed," used above, it should not be inferred that the constituents of the sphere of form are necessarily diminutive and weak in the sense sphere. On the contrary, they are the main elements in many types of sense consciousness, and for the purposes of that sphere four of them may be quite strongly developed. It is mainly the fifth factor, mental one-pointedness, that needs to be specially cultivated in order to acquire the intensity required for the meditative absorptions; and, of course, a change in the *direction* of all the factors is necessary.

Starting from the degree of strength that the factors of absorption possess in an average state of consciousness, a further intensification of consciousness aiming at realization of the Noble Eightfold Path may proceed in any of three directions: (1) emphasis on thought and examination (*vitakka-vicāra*) leads to an intensification of the intellectual faculties to be directed toward the growth of insight (*vipassanā*); (2) emphasis on mental one-pointedness leads to the attainment of full absorption (*appanā* or *jhāna*); (3) when the fourth jhāna has been mastered, the four dominant factors (*adhipati*; i.e., intention, energy, consciousness, and investigation) may be developed into the four "roads to power" (*iddhipāda*). Here the intensity of consciousness is increased to a degree sufficient to grant access to the psychic powers (*iddhividha*), giving the practitioner a far-reaching control over mind and matter.[41] As mentioned already, this psychic control of matter may be viewed as an extension of a feature of the factors of absorption in their general aspects as intensifying factors, namely, that owing to their presence consciousness is enabled to produce certain corporeal phenomena (see p. 53).

On the other hand, as already mentioned, the possibilities latent in the average human consciousness may also lead downward to rebirth in the animal realm. The fact that all the intensifying factors, more or less developed, may be present in higher animals implies both that human beings can sink down to the animal level and that animals can rise up to the human level. If human consciousness did not share certain features in common with the lower and the higher worlds, rebirth as an animal or in the celestial spheres would not be possible.

The intensity of a state of consciousness does not allow anything to be said about its ethical value or its spiritual rank. It is a point common to the intensifying factors and the pentad of sense-contact that both groups are ethically indifferent; they may occur in wholesome, unwholesome, and kammically neutral consciousness. Both groups take, as it were, the color of their "root sap," that is, they assume the quality of the wholesome, unwholesome, or neutral "root causes" (*mūla* or *hetu*) associated with them. One of the differences between these two groups is that the pentad contains only constant factors, while among the factors of absorption there also appear, for the first time in our list, nonconstant ones that are not present in every type of consciousness, namely, thought, examination, and rapture (*vitakka, vicāra, pīti*).

4. The Faculties *(indriya, F11–18)*

Next comes a group of eight factors called *indriya.* Their common function consists in exercising a dominating, governing, or controlling influence over the other mental factors associated with them and over simultaneously arisen corporeal phenomena. This function is indicated in the commentaries by reference to the derivation of the word *indriya* from *inda* (Skt *indra*), "lord"; for example, "Faith exercises lordship under the sign of resolution."[42] Like *jhāna, indriya* too is one of the twenty-four modes of conditionality (*paccaya*). The faculties are said to be *indriya* "in the sense of lordship called predominance."[43] Relying on these traditional explanations, we may call the *indriyas* "controlling factors," though we shall also retain the somewhat vague name of "faculties" most often used in translations.

First in order of enumeration is a subgroup of five factors beginning with the faculty of faith that we shall call "the five spiritual faculties." Of these, besides the general definition mentioned above, an additional explanation of their *indriya*-nature is given by the commentators: they are called *indriyas* because "they master their opposites,"[44] that is, they keep them under control. Faith (F11) brings faithlessness under control; energy (F12) controls indolence; mindfulness (F13) controls heedlessness; concentration (F14) controls agitation; and wisdom (F15) controls ignorance.[45] These five spiritual faculties occur so frequently in the Sutta Piṭaka that we need not give any sutta references for them.

The sixth place in that group is occupied by the faculty of mind (*manindriya,* F16). It belongs to the six sense faculties and is identical with the factor "consciousness" (*citta,* F5) in the pentad of sense-contact. Mind is a controlling faculty on account of its preeminent position among the mental factors (*cetasika*) associated with it. These latter factors, among them also the other faculties, by fulfilling their own particular tasks, serve at the same time the purpose of the general function of consciousness or mind (*citta, mano, viññāṇa*), which consists in discriminating (*vijānana*) the object.

Besides, in the sense of the already given general definition of *indriya,* there is also implied the control exercised by mind over certain corporeal phenomena. An example of that control is the conscious intention accompanying and directing purposeful bodily movements (= *kāyaviññatti*) and vocal utterance (= *vacīviññatti*). This *indriya*-quality of consciousness, as manifested in a certain control over matter, is capable of far-reaching development. It reaches its peak in one of the four roads to power (*iddhipāda*). The efficacy attributed to it is illustrated by the following passage in the Iddhikathā chapter of the *Paṭisambhidāmagga*: "If he wishes to resort to the Brahma-world with his body remaining invisible, then he forces the body by his consciousness, he directs the body by his consciousness."[46] Neither the *cittasamādhi-iddhipāda* nor the corresponding *cittadhipati* ("predominance of consciousness") is sufficiently explained in the texts or the commentaries. It is, however, rather easier to understand how such a powerful influence could be ascribed to the other three constituents of these two groups, that is, intention, energy, and investigation. But now, with our reference to the general *indriya*-quality of consciousness, that is, its controlling power, we hope to have contributed to a better understanding of the role of consciousness too. It will now be clearer how the "mere fact of being conscious" can achieve such prominence as a "predominant factor" (*adhipati*) or a "road to power" (*iddhipāda*). It is the *manindriya*-aspect of consciousness, namely, its controlling power, that is the starting point of these developments. In this connection, it should be recalled that the ancient teachers expressly define *indriya* by *adhipacca* (being the abstract form of *adhipati*), that is, predominance or sovereignty.

With this brief excursion into the "realm of magic" we have tried to show that the inclusion of the controlling aspect of consciousness is justified not only by its normal influence over mental and corporeal phenomena, but also because it represents one of the starting points of higher development inherent in normal consciousness. Of course, not only the faculty of mind, but the five spiritual faculties and the intensifying factors of absorption as well, form the foundation on which the lofty structure of spiritually developed consciousness can be built. But it is of particular interest that such an active part in that development is ascribed to "mere consciousness." Obviously, these ancient Buddhist thinkers clearly comprehended (without formulating it in the abstract) that developed consciousness represents an eminently activating and mobilizing force against the tendencies to stagnation and inertia of nature in general and of the human mind in particular. They have pointed to that aspect of consciousness (*citta*) by defining it as *citta* (= *citra*)-*karaṇa*, "that which makes for differentiation" (see p. 46). This activating, and thereby governing, influence of consciousness is due to its *manindriya*-aspect, that is, consciousness considered as a controlling faculty; or, we might say, it is due to "conscious control."[47] This general aspect of consciousness forms the basis on which other activating and controlling factors, such as mindfulness (*sati*), etc., might be successfully cultivated. With their help the field of conscious control might be extended far beyond the imagination of those who have lost sight of the ideal of Man Perfected or of that type of superman (*mahāpurisa*) that the Buddha defines as the embodiment of perfect mindfulness (*sati*) and perfect clarity of consciousness (*sampajañña*).[48]

Returning to our subject proper, we repeat that the above examples show that the apparent repetitions in the List of Dhammas are not superfluous but serve to highlight essential aspects as well as potentialities of the respective mental factor. Careful consideration of these aspects and potentialities will yield important aids to a deeper understanding of the theory and practice of the Buddha's doctrine.

We can now resume our cursory treatment of the eight faculties. The seventh, the *faculty of joy* (*somanassindriya*, F17), belongs to the five faculties relating to feeling, namely, bodily pleasure, bodily pain, joy, grief, and indifference. Joy is an *indriya*, a controlling faculty, because when a joyful mood arises it dominates one's whole being. It suffuses all the other associated mental qualities (e.g., the intellectual activity), giving them a mood of joyfulness, and it enlivens the accompanying bodily activity as well. Grief and indifference too appear as controlling faculties in the respective classes of consciousness. It need not be elaborated here how sadness (or aversion, which likewise counts as *domanassa*, "grief") and indifference (or equipoise) influence or control mental and bodily activities.

The eighth faculty is that of *vitality* (*jīvitindriya*, F18), which represents the life force of mental phenomena, as distinct from the identically named factor that governs physical vitality and has its place among the constituents of corporeality (*rūpakkhandha*). The faculty of psychic vitality controls and guards the continuance of the mental life process.

Among the faculties there appear (for the first time in the list) factors that occur only in good consciousness.[49] These faculties are faith, mindfulness, and wisdom. The ethical value of the remaining two spiritual faculties, concentration and energy, is variable. The faculty of concentration is identical with mental one-pointedness in the factors of absorption. Energy appears here for the first time.

In order to perform their governing and controlling functions the faculties require a high degree of strength and intensity, which is imparted to them by the intensifying factors of absorption. It is therefore consistent that the controlling faculties are preceded in the list by the intensifying factors of absorption, which are their supporting conditions. The following examples illustrate the connection between these two groups, exemplifying at the same time the "internal relations" mentioned above (p. 23).

Faith, devotion or confidence, has a controlling or governing influence on the character only if the factors of absorption *pīti*—that is, rapture, joyful interest, or enthusiasm—and *sukha*—pleasure or happiness—themselves possess a considerable degree of intensity, and in their above-mentioned function impart it to faith as well. It is from joy that faith derives a good part of its conquering power; and it is keen and enthusiastic interest that makes for the constancy of faith or devotion. Furthermore, faith is able to become exclusive devotion only if there is also a high degree of mental one-pointedness to perform the intensifying function of a *jhānaṅga*.

For the faculty of wisdom to comprehend its objects fully, keenness of intellect must be highly developed by the two intensifying factors, thought (*vitakka*) and examination (*vicāra*). For the spiritual faculties of energy, mindfulness, and concentration to unfold, a high degree of stimulating interest (*pīti*) is required in order to intensify their activity. On the other hand, when mindfulness and concentration are progressing well, their part is to sustain and increase interest by preventing it from fading away.

The mind faculty, in its general function of control over the cognitive process and in its inherent potentiality for greater alertness, lucidity, and power, is helped by the intensifying effect of all five factors of absorption, particularly mental one-pointedness.

The faculty of joy is identical with the factor of absorption pleasure (*sukha*), but it is stronger and more enduring when linked to a high degree of intensifying *pīti* with the grades of interest, enthusiasm, and rapture. In the suttas, *pīti* often forms a compound with either *somanassa* or *sukha*.

The faculty of psychic vitality, too, is enlivened by interest and transmits this intensifying effect, received from joyful interest, to physical vitality as well. For example, as any physician will confirm, in old or sick people vivid interests in persons, affairs, or ideas may prolong life by giving the incentive to muster all physical and mental powers of resistance. On the other hand, it happens just as often that old or sick people deteriorate quickly when they "lose interest in life," owing, for example, to the death of a beloved person or to a disappointment.

The five spiritual faculties together with the corresponding five spiritual powers (dealt with in the next section) continue the work begun by the factors of absorption. They increase the agility and pliancy of the mind and its capacity to effect deliberate inner changes, whether positive, negative, or adaptive. These last features are the basis for any mental and spiritual progress. It is mainly owing to the operation of these five spiritual faculties and powers that noticeable transformations of character, conduct, ideas, and ideals are made possible. Sometimes they even seem capable of bringing about a complete metamorphosis of the personality. One can cite, for example, the vast inner and outer changes, or the "revaluation of all values," occurring in the lives of the great religious figures after they received their "revelations" or discovered their mission.

If, to the contrary, the intensifying and controlling factors are weak or partly absent, a general heaviness and unwieldiness of the mental processes results: force of habit predominates; changes and adaptations are undertaken slowly and unwillingly, and to the smallest possible degree; thought is rigid, inclining to dogma. Such people learn from experience or advice only slowly; their affections and aversions are fixed and biased; and in general their character is more or less intractable. In such a condition the human mind veers dangerously close to the level of the higher animals with their very limited mental agility; for in them too the intensifying factors may be partly present, but only in a very weak degree (see pp. 55-57). It is owing to the fixity and unwieldiness as well as to the weakness of the animal mind that, as the Buddha often pointed out, the emergence of a being from the animal kingdom to a rebirth in the human world is so exceedingly difficult.

We have dealt in detail with the positive and beneficial side of the controlling power wielded by the five spiritual faculties over the other mental factors. But such power also has a negative, or at least a somewhat dangerous, aspect: namely, the controlling influence of these faculties may develop to an excessive degree. If a single faculty is developed exclusively while the others, especially the counterparts, are neglected or deliberately suppressed, that faculty may come to exercise unbridled control over the entire personality. For example, if allowed to grow at the expense of the rest, faith (*saddhā*), reason (*paññā*), energy (*viriya*), and concentration (*samādhi*), may each seriously impair and weaken the others. As in the macrocosm of human society so in the microcosm of the human mind, those in charge are often tempted to abuse their power. In both cases the final result is bad: balance is disturbed and an obstacle sets in to continuous and harmonious development. This shows the importance as well as the wisdom of insisting on the "harmony of the five spiritual faculties" (*indriya-samatta*) as taught by the Buddha and elaborated in the commentaries.[50] It is the faculty of mindfulness (*satindriya*) that watches over the harmonization of the other four faculties, and so has the "chief control" over the other controlling factors.

5. THE POWERS *(bala, F24–30)*

We have already remarked how the faculty of controlling presupposes a certain intensity of the mental factors concerned. We have seen how the function of intensifying is performed by the factors of absorption, and we have given examples of this in the particular case of the five spiritual faculties. The resultant intensity of those faculties is described and emphasized by repeating them in the list under the name of powers (*bala*).

The commentarial explanation (e.g., at *Asl* 124) says that the five factors corresponding to the spiritual faculties, and also the two additional constituents of this group, namely moral shame (*hiri*) and moral dread (*ottappa*), are called "powers" because they are "unshakable" (*akampiya*) by their opposites; thus, for example, faith is not shaken by faithlessness (or unbelief). But in view of the fact that all these psychological statements refer in the first instance only to the duration of a single moment of consciousness, and since the "control" or "power" won at that moment may well be lost in the next, it is better and less ambitious to render the word *akampiya* by "firm." So we may say that these seven factors are powers of firm preponderance. In the case of the five spiritual faculties, this signifies that the "control" exercised by them has gained a degree of stability.

It should be borne in mind that the five spiritual faculties and the five spiritual powers are simply two different aspects of the same qualities. How their nature is basically one, though their functions are different, was illustrated by the Buddha in the following simile: If there was a river flowing eastward with an island in the midst of it, the stream could be regarded as one when seen in its flow at the eastern and western sides of the island, but as two from the island's northern and southern sides. In the same way should the identity of the spiritual faculties and powers be understood (*SN* V 219–20).

When the function of these five powers is considered within a single moment, merely the somewhat self-evident fact is implied that in order to be in existence at all the corresponding five spiritual faculties must necessarily have been able to "overpower" the opposing tendencies for the duration of that moment (their *indriya*-quality), and that by doing so they have achieved a certain "firmness" (their *bala*-quality) for that period. The powers can be said to be present to that extent even when the faculties are relatively weak. But this does not exhaust the power-aspect. They are not only those limited actualities of the brief present moment but also potentialities for the future. We have already mentioned that the enumeration of a factor under different group headings points to potential connections with such other constituents of these groups as are not included in the given state of consciousness; in other words, new perspectives are opened up beyond the present moment. In that case, the potentialities refer to an increasing width of relations with other wholesome factors.

Here in the case of the spiritual powers the potentialities included in that aspect refer to strength increasing to the degree that these powers become "unshakable" (*akampiya*) in the full sense of the word. This takes place on the attainment of the four supramundane paths (*ariyamagga*), the stages of awakening. Only then, when certain fetters (*saṁyojana*) and hindrances (*nīvaraṇa*) have been completely abolished, do those faculties and other spiritual qualities too become really "unshakable," so that they can no more be lost. For example, faith becomes "unshakable" when the fetter or hindrance of doubt (*vicikicchā*) is radically destroyed on reaching the stage of stream-entry (*sotāpatti*). So for the practical purpose of spiritual development the mention of the power-aspect may serve as an incentive not to be satisfied with the spiritual faculties' exercise of momentary or short-lived control or power, but to strive untiringly until they have reached the full status of "unshakable powers."

If we consider the potentialities and not only the limited actualities, we can say that the power-aspect of these five factors, though actually present in the given moment, need not be as strongly developed as the controlling (*indriya*) aspect. This is corroborated by the fact that in certain types of consciousness the power-aspect may be quite absent, though the faculty-aspect is present. We shall discuss this in greater detail below (§15).

The last two powers given in the list are *moral shame* (*hiri*, F29) and *moral dread* (*ottappa*, F30). They strengthen wholesome consciousness making it "unshakable" by shamelessness and unscrupulousness. If their roots go deep enough in the character of the individual, they will automatically set up spontaneous reactions of restraint and curb all evil influences. Therefore, in the repeated occurrence that follows in the list (F37, 38) these two powers are called "the guardians of the world" (see §9). They are indispensable for securing, protecting, and stabilizing moral qualities and are therefore the prerequisites of further spiritual growth. While in general we called the factors of this group "powers of firm preponderance," these two in particular may be called "protective powers." Owing to their purely "defensive" function, they have no counterpart among the more active *indriyas*, as the other five powers have.

6. The Path Factors *(magganga, F19–23)*

In the actual order of the list the path factors are placed before the powers, which we preferred to explain immediately after the spiritual faculties on account of their close connection with them.

Only five of the factors of the Noble Eightfold Path are given in the list. The remaining three, namely, right speech, right action, and right livelihood, are not included because they are variable factors, that is, they do not *necessarily* appear in every instance of this type of consciousness, and they do not arise together at the same moment. They are included in the supplementary factors (*ye-vā-panaka*), under the names of abstinence from evil conduct in words, deeds, and livelihood.

Of the path factors given specifically, four are identical with—or better, different aspects of—the corresponding spiritual faculties (*indriya*):

right view (F19)	=	faculty of wisdom (F15)
right effort (F21)	=	faculty of energy (F12)
right mindfulness (F22)	=	faculty of mindfulness (F13)
right concentration (F23)	=	faculty of concentration (F14)

The fifth, right thought (*sammā-saṅkappa*, F20), is counted as a repeated enumeration of the factor of absorption "thought" (*vitakka*, F6).

If we search for a reason why, in the arrangement of the list, the path factors are enumerated after the faculties, we may find it perhaps in the fact that the path factors continue the work of the spiritual faculties in effecting a stronger *directive* or *purposive* energy within the flow of wholesome consciousness—a tendency already prominent in the spiritual faculties, as we have seen. But as was mentioned earlier, the four spiritual faculties when not harmonized tend to dominate and to suppress their counterparts, and there lies the danger that they will lose to some extent their original measure of directive energy. Their function can easily become a purpose in itself and an enjoyment in itself. The goal toward which the particular faculty was originally working and moving will lose its importance, and so its directive influence on that faculty and on the entire personality will diminish. It can even happen that the original goal is easily replaced by its opposite. For example, the strong urge felt by some people to "believe in something" (= *saddhindriya*) may cause them to change with surprising facility the object of their belief. Or a keen intellect (= *paññindriya*), enjoying its versatility and superiority, may all too soon be ready to "prove" just the opposite of what it had advocated a while ago; this leads to intellectual dishonesty and to indifference or cynicism with regard to spiritual values. We know, besides, how a fervid thirst for unceasing activity (= *viriyindriya*) tries to quench itself in sundry ways, often very indiscriminately chosen. These examples show how great the danger can be that arises from the dominating tendency of the *indriyas.* It can be countered (1) by their harmonization (see p. 63), and (2) by emphasizing their aspect as path factors that is inherent in them. If one constantly remembers that the noblest use of those faculties is in the service of the liberating path, then they will be less liable to go astray.

With the path factors we enter the sphere of definite and unmistakable values and value-attributions, and their directive and purposive energy is consequently greater than that of the spiritual faculties. Hence the commentary (*Asl* 154) explains the path factors as "factors of deliverance" (*niyyānaṭṭhena,* lit. "leading out," i.e., from saṁsāra), and as "conditions" (*hetu-aṭṭhena*), that is, as conditions or requirements for the attainment of arahantship. For example, the factor "concentration" (= mental one-pointedness) is in itself neutral, that is, outside the sphere of values, but if it receives the value-attribution "right" (*sammā*), it then becomes a path factor, a factor of deliverance; for from the highest standpoint of the Buddhist doctrine only what is conducive to deliverance is called "right."

However, the path-factor quality of a certain mental concomitant is not necessarily quite distinct in every occurrence of the type of wholesome consciousness concerned; still less is there always a conscious awareness of it. The knowledge associated (*ñāṇasampayutta*) with the first type of wholesome consciousness (dealt with here) may not always be strongly developed, being frequently limited to the immediate occasion of that thought without looking beyond it. Besides, the individual concerned need not necessarily be acquainted at all with the Noble Eightfold Path and its goal. Nevertheless, the path-factor aspect is actually present in those cases too, signifying at the very least a minute contribution to the process of preparing a way to deliverance.

We now add a few remarks on interrelation and cooperation between the last two groups and the path factors.

The *indriya*-quality supports the path-quality of the corresponding factors through its controlling and thereby coordinating influence on the other simultaneous mental concomitants and bodily activities, making them subservient to the liberating purpose of the path and engaging them, as it were, as auxiliary workers for "preparing the way."

The *power*-quality, having the nature of being "unshakable" by opposite qualities, supports the path-aspect by its "preponderant influence" in keeping "the way" free from obstruction and preventing deviations, thus ensuring a firm and steady course.

On the other hand, if the character as a *path factor* is strongly marked and highly developed in the corresponding faculties and powers, arbitrariness in their application to other purposes will be reduced and eventually abolished; they will be less threatened by separation and disruption caused by a lack of balance; they will be directed more purposefully to deliverance as the sole salutary goal.

The inclusion of the path factors in the analysis of wholesome consciousness means the raising of the spiritual eye from the narrow confines and limited purposes of everyday consciousness to the horizon of the ideal. It means that, in the midst of life's dense jungle, amid its labyrinths and blind alleys, the glorious freedom of a Way is open. It means the gradual liberation of the mind from skeptical or muddled aimlessness by pointing to a well-marked Way leading to a definite and noble destination. Already from the mere awareness that such a Way does exist and that it is traceable in the wholesome thought arising right now, there comes assurance and peace, solace and encouragement. The path factors are an appeal to make every moment of one's life a part of the Great Way and to continue in that effort until the goal is near and its attainment assured, until the Way is transfigured into the supramundane path (*lokuttara-magga*).

7. The Wholesome Roots *(kusala-mūla, F31–33)*

The three wholesome roots are the main criteria by which a state of consciousness is determined to be wholesome. The first two, non-greed (*alobha*) and non-hate (*adosa*), are present in every class of kammically wholesome consciousness. Non-delusion (*amoha*) is found only in those wholesome states of consciousness that are "associated with knowledge" (*ñāṇasampayutta*).

Non-greed and non-hate appear here for the first time in the list and occur once more later on among the "ways of wholesome action" (F34, 35). Non-delusion was earlier represented in the list by other aspects (F15, 19, 28), and it occurs three times more (F36, 52, 54).

Non-greed and non-hate may, according to the particular case, have either a mainly negative meaning signifying absence of greed and hate, or they may possess a distinctly positive character: for example, non-greed as renunciation, liberality; non-hate as amity, kindness, forbearance. Non-delusion always has a positive meaning, for it represents the knowledge that motivates the particular state of consciousness. In their positive aspects, non-greed and non-hatred are likewise strong motives of good actions. They supply the nonrational, volitional, or emotional motives, while non-delusion represents the rational motive of a good thought or action.

The three roots may be called "motive powers," in the double sense of these words, since they induce and impel the other simultaneously arisen mental factors to act in the service of that motive. Their "root sap" actuates and nourishes these other factors and gives the "color" of a wholesome quality to factors that are in themselves "colorless," that is, neutral.

The wholesome roots too belong to the "sphere of values," but they do not necessarily have the strong purposefulness of the path factors or their invariable directedness toward the goal of deliverance. Like the spiritual faculties, they may in many instances be entirely limited to the particular occasion.

Common membership in the "sphere of values" seems to be the only connection between the wholesome roots and the preceding group of path factors, as well as the following "ways of action."

8. The Ways of Action *(kammapatha, F34–36)*

The same three wholesome roots, though differently named, now reappear again in their aspect of wholesome ways of action. Here they are called non-covetousness (*anabhijjhā*), non-ill will (*avyāpāda*), and right view (*sammā-diṭṭhi*). They comprise mental action or *kamma*, and they alone among all the ten ways of action enter this analysis of consciousness. The remaining seven ways of action refer to the actual performance of bodily and verbal actions and therefore do not enter into an analysis of consciousness. Only the volitions combined with them might be thought to be included in the supplementary factors, abstinence from wrong bodily and verbal action (F63, 64).

While these three factors, if considered as roots, belong to the "impelling" or "motive powers" of the unceasingly turning Wheel of Life, they are here regarded as sections of that wheel insofar as it moves on a wholesome course of action. Thus they belong to the formative powers (*abhisaṅkhāra*) of a happy rebirth. They and their unwholesome counterparts are treated in detail in the *Atthasālinī.*

9. The Guardians of the World *(lokapāla, F37, 38)*

This group comprises the two factors moral shame (*hiri*) and moral dread (*ottappa*). In their first enumeration as "powers" (F29, 30; see p. 65-66), they may be regarded as guardians of the self, that is, as protectors of the wholesome character of the other mental factors arising at the same moment. That means that they refer, in that instance, mainly to the inner world and to individual ethics. Here, in their character as guardians of the world, their relation to the outer world is emphasized. They appear here as the pillars of social ethics, the guardians and regulators of the relations between the individual and society. The presence of moral shame and moral dread in each wholesome moment of consciousness forms a protection against the deterioration of humankind's moral standards. They are, as it were, the brakes of our mind-vehicle and the restraining forces against their opposites, shamelessness and unscrupulousness. The more spontaneous and strong the voice of shame and conscience is in its individual members, the less force and coercion is required to maintain a high moral level in society. Therefore these two qualities were rightly called by the Buddha "guardians of the world."[51]

No inner connection of this group with the preceding one and the subsequent one can apparently be established. This holds true also of the groups that follow.

10. The Six Pairs of Qualitative Factors *(yugalakāni, F39–50)*

The twelve factors, beginning with "tranquillity of mental concomitants" (*kāya-passaddhi*, F39), always arise together. They occur only in good consciousness (see note 49) and are common to all types of it (*sobhana-sādhāraṇa*). In the *Atthasālinī* they are sometimes called "the six pairs" (*cha yugalakāni*) for short. We shall now describe them singly by way of their own distinctive features and through their opposites, drawing upon the analysis provided by the Abhidhamma commentaries.[52]

Description of the Six Pairs

1. *Tranquillity* is the quiet, equable, and composed condition, firstly of consciousness in general (*citta-passaddhi*, F40), and secondly of its single concomitant factors (*kāya-passaddhi*, F39). It therefore refers (1) to the tranquil "keynote" of the mind, and (2) to the quiet, smooth, and even functioning of the mental factors, undisturbed by agitation and restlessness. According to the *Atthasālinī*, it is opposed

to anxiety (*daratha*) and to the hindrance of agitation (*uddhacca*). We may add that in its aspect of a "good conscience" it is also opposed to the hindrance of worry (*kukkucca*) due to bad conscience or scruples. As to the influence of tranquillity on single mental factors, we shall give only two examples: (1) In the case of joy (*sukha, somanassindriya*), the presence of tranquillity means that joy will be a "tranquil happiness" without admixture of agitation (*uddhacca*), which would render it unwholesome (*akusala*). (2) Energy (*viriyindriya*), in connection with tranquillity, will be a "quiet strength" displaying itself in a well-balanced, measured, and therefore effective way, without boisterousness or uncontrolled exuberance, which spends itself quickly and often in vain.

Within the sensuous sphere (*kāmāvacara*), tranquillity is the inner peace bestowed by any moral act or thought, that is, the peace of an unruffled conscience. It is also equability of the mental functions necessary for effective work in the field of insight (*vipassanā*), making, for example, for an unwavering and cool, reliable, and dispassionate judgment. The *Atthasālinī* says: "The manifestation of tranquillity is the unwavering and cool state (*aparipphandanasītibhāva*) of consciousness and its concomitants."

Beyond that, as a prior condition for the factors of absorption happiness (*sukha*) and mental one-pointedness (*cittass'ekaggatā*), tranquillity prepares the way for entry into the jhānic consciousness of the sphere of form (*rūpāvacara*). Thus in the suttas, in the stock passage describing the preparatory stage of the jhānas (e.g., at *DN* I 73), it is said: "being tranquil in body, he experiences happiness; the mind of one who is happy becomes concentrated."

Finally, tranquillity is the seed, present in every wholesome consciousness, that can grow to full stature in the tranquillity factor of enlightenment (*passaddhi-sambojjhaṅga*), which, when perfected, belongs to supramundane consciousness (*lokuttara-citta*).

2. *Agility* (*lahutā*, lit. "lightness") of wholesome states of consciousness refers to one of the fundamental qualities of mind in general: its "lightness" and mobility that distinguishes it from heavy and inert matter. Agility of good consciousness signifies (1) buoyancy of the mental condition in general (*citta-lahutā*, F42), and

"the capacity of the mind to turn very quickly to a wholesome object or to the contemplation of impermanence, etc." (*DhsMṭ* 97). (2) In the case of the single mental factors (*kāya-lahutā*, F41), it signifies the swiftness of their functions: their capacity to act and to react quickly, for example, to seize at once an occasion to do a good deed or to grasp quickly the implications of a thought or a situation. It is the basis for such qualities as presence of mind, ready wit, etc.

Agility is said to be the opposite of the hindrance or defilement of rigidity and sloth (*thīna-middha*), which causes heaviness (*garutā*) and hardness (*thaddhabhāva*); that is, it is opposed to a general sluggishness, dullness, and apathy of consciousness as well as to slowness of its various functions, which causes, for example, slowness of apprehension or response intellectually as well as emotionally. A noteworthy passage in the *Mūlaṭīkā* (p. 97) says that "agility is the enabling condition for swift emergence from the subconscious life-continuum (*bhavaṅga-vuṭṭhāna*)."

3. *Pliancy* (*mudutā*, lit. "softness") is the susceptibility, elasticity, resilience, and adaptability of the mind, which bestow on the mind a greater and more durable efficiency, a "sounder health,"[53] than it could be expected to possess when in a rigid state. "Soft conquers hard," says Lao-tse. It should also be remembered how often mental insanity is associated with an excessive rigidity or lack of pliancy or resilience of the mind. If this factor refers to the condition of mind in general, it is called "pliancy of consciousness" (*citta-mudutā*, F44).

Pliancy of the concomitants (*kāya-mudutā*, F43) consists, for example, in adaptability of the respective functions to their various tasks. It is, moreover, a high impressionability or sensitivity in the perceptive and cognitive faculties and in moral emotion. It is the capacity of the intellectual faculties to learn and to unlearn ever anew, to be benefitted by experience. It allows one to discard inveterate habits and prejudices pertaining to thought, emotion, and behavior. It contributes to the devotion and self-surrender in faith (*saddhā*), to the gentleness and forgiveness in non-hate (*adosa*) or love (*mettā*). Due to its aspect of sensitive susceptibility it also increases the mind's imaginative capacity, an important factor in the development of intuition.

Agility and pliancy may be regarded as a counterpart to tranquillity. The commentator cites "anxiety" (*daratha*) as one of the defilements particularly countered by tranquillity. We venture to introduce here the canonical term *khila* (barrenness, obstruction, stoppage) as the opposite of pliancy and as a counterpart of *daratha.* Here, in these negative counterparts, the expectant tension of "anxiety" stands against the oppressive dullness of being hopelessly obstructed. The commentary expressly names as opposites the defilements *diṭṭhi* (which here may be rendered best as "dogmatism" or "opinionatedness") and *māna* (conceit). Both defilements are said to cause hardness or inflexibility (*thaddhabhāva*). As opposed to dogmatic rigidity, pliancy appears as open-mindedness. Conceit and any other egocentric hardenings of the heart are countered by pliancy in its aspects of humane accessibility to others, appreciation of others, and making allowance for them. The manifestation of pliancy is said to be non-resistance (*appaṭighāta*), which may refer, for example, to the "non-resistance" to appeals (or impulses) to selfless action, or to readiness to yield in argument.

Pliancy of mind counteracts any tendency in the human character and intellect to become rigid; it widens the boundaries of the so-called ego by admitting into it new elements from the world of non-ego; it is a prerequisite for true tolerance that includes understanding.

4. *Workableness* (*kammaññatā,* F45, 46) is that medium consistency, or that tempered state, of consciousness and its concomitants, in which neither firmness nor softness is excessive. Perfect "workableness" of mind means that these two qualities, firmness and softness, are in the right proportion to permit the greatest efficiency of the mental functions and to suit best the formative and transformative work of spiritual development (*bhāvanā*). This is how the *Mūlaṭīkā* expresses it (p. 97): "Workableness signifies that specific or suitable degree of pliancy or softness (*mudutā-visiṭṭhā,* or *anurūpa-mudutā*) which makes the gold—that is, the mind—workable. While the mind is in the flames of passion it is too soft to be workable, as molten gold is. If, on the contrary, the mind is too rigid then it is comparable to untempered gold."

Excessive rigidity of mind, being insufficiently impressionable, resists any attempt to transform or reform it. On the other hand, excessive pliancy makes the mind too impressionable, and with the mind in such a condition impressions are not retained long enough to leave any noticeable effect but are soon obliterated by new ones.

So it is most important, for anyone aiming at an effective transformation of consciousness through spiritual training, to achieve, as perfectly as possible for a beginner, that medium quality of mind implied in the term "workableness."

The *Atthasālinī* says that the opposites of workableness are "all those remaining hindrances that render consciousness and its concomitants unwieldy." This may refer particularly to sensual desire (*kāmacchanda*) and hate (*vyāpāda*). Sensual desire "softens" the mind, makes it "shapeless," effaces its characteristic contours, dilutes and dissolves. Hate (aversion, resentment, etc.) represents the other extreme: it hardens, contracts, imprisons, alienates. Therefore, in proportion to the achievement of that medium state of workableness, the mind will be assisted in uprooting the two unwholesome roots of lust and hate.

5. *Proficiency* (*pāguññatā*, F47, 48) is, according to the *Dhammasaṅgaṇī*, fitness and competence of mind and mental factors. According to the *Atthasālinī*, it is opposed to their "sickliness" (*gelaññabhāva*), caused by such defilements as lack of faith or confidence (*asaddhiya*), etc. That is to say, it is opposed to feebleness of the mental and moral constitution and to inefficiency, which appear also as inner uncertainty and lack of self-confidence. The commentarial explanation by "sickliness" points again to the meaning of *kusala* as "moral and mental health."

Inner certainty, assurance, and efficiency in the doing of a good deed, which are expressed by the factor proficiency, are increased in proportion to the repeated performance of that act, resulting in its spontaneity. Generally, it can be said that all these last-mentioned five pairs, and particularly proficiency, are more highly developed in those good states of consciousness classed as "spontaneous" (*asaṅkhārena*).

6. *Uprightness* (*ujukatā*, F49, 50) is opposed to insincerity, hypocrisy, etc. This factor prevents a state of consciousness from being called "good" when selfish secondary motives are hidden behind thoughts, words, and deeds of moral significance. The inclusion of the

factor uprightness serves to emphasize that the ethical—that is, kammic—quality of a state of consciousness is determined only by an unambiguous intention (*cetanā*). An example will make this clearer and will also show how the abstract but penetrative analysis of the Abhidhamma may be used for the practical purpose of an introspective scrutiny of motives. Let us suppose that a charitable act has the secondary, or even the primary, object of winning fame for the donor. Then that moment of consciousness in which the selfish motive appears will be kammically unwholesome, being rooted in greed and delusion. But the state of consciousness accompanying the actual performance of the charitable act will be kammically wholesome, because the actual relinquishing of the object to be given away will generally imply non-greed. This type of consciousness would probably have the following classification: "without (right) knowledge," because inspired by desire for fame; "nonspontaneous," because preceded by deliberation referring to a secondary motive; probably emotionally "indifferent," because there will scarcely be much joy in such a case. With these classifications, the thought in question is included in the eighth type of wholesome consciousness, which is also the last and lowest in quality, though in the case of other types the order of enumeration does not always represent an order of value.

Interrelations among the Six Pairs

The following examples may suffice to illustrate the mutual relations among the six pairs.

Tranquillity and agility balance each other: tranquillity has a moderating influence on agility, and agility a stimulating influence on tranquillity.

As we have seen, pliancy is a fundamental condition of workableness, while the requirements of the latter set a limit to the degree of pliancy or softness desirable.

Uprightness prevents the agility and pliancy of mind from falling into insincerity, while agility and pliancy take care that uprightness does not grow unimaginative and rigid and thereby impair the adaptability of wholesome consciousness to actuality.

Proficiency gives agility that sureness and smoothness of movement which comes from long practice. On the other hand, agility, implying the capacity to admit of modifications and changes, prevents proficiency from becoming an overspecialized and inflexible habit, and so limiting the adaptability as well as the potentialities of the mind.

Verification of the Six Pairs in the Suttas

Only the pair of proficiency appears untraceable in the suttas. The abstract noun *pāguññatā* does not, to our knowledge, occur there at all. The adjective *paguṇa*, being more characteristic of later Pāli literature, is met only very rarely in the Sutta Piṭaka and in such irrelevant contexts that the Abhidhamma term has certainly not been derived from these passages. It is possible that the use of the words *kusala* and *kusalatā* in the suttas to mean "skillful" (e.g., *khandhakusala*, "skillful in the aggregates") may have contributed to the inclusion of that mental factor in the List of Dhammas, though under a different name.

We have already observed (p. 71-72) how *tranquillity* occurs in the suttas as a condition for the factor of absorption "happiness" and as a factor of enlightenment (*bojjhaṅga*). In explaining the latter, *SN* V 107 mentions both kinds of tranquillity: "Monks, there is tranquillity of the mental factors (*kāya-passaddhi*) and tranquillity of consciousness (*citta-passaddhi*)."

Agility, or lightness (*lahutā*) of mind in general, is referred to in the following passage: "Monks, I do not know of any one thing that is as lightly changing (*lahuparivattaṁ*) as the mind (*cittaṁ*)" (*AN* I 10). This passage has certainly influenced the definition of our mental factor *lahutā* (at *Dhs* §42) by *lahupariṇāmitā*, which is synonymous with the sutta term *lahuparivattaṁ*. The context of that brief statement from the Aṅguttara Nikāya suggests that the phrase refers not only to the general idea of the transitoriness of mind but also to the particular aspect of the mind's susceptibility to quick transformation and modification, a quality useful to moral and spiritual development. This quotation is in fact preceded by the well-known passage: "O monks, I do not know of any one thing that, if developed and cultivated, is as pliant (*mudu*) and workable (*kammaññu*) as the mind." Therefore we feel justified in quoting the former passage as a source of the term.

An increased feeling of lightness (*lahukasaññā*) is mentioned as being present when the Buddha employed his supernormal powers: "Ānanda, when the Exalted One subordinates the body to the mind, or the mind to the body, and a feeling of happiness and lightness descends on the body, at that time, Ānanda, the body of the Exalted One is lighter (*lahutaro*) and more pliant (*mudutaro*), more workable (*kammaniyataro*) and more luminous (*pabhassarataro*)" (*SN* V 283). In this passage and the previous one we find other terms belonging to the six pairs. We shall refer to these quotations again just below.

Uprightness is frequently mentioned in the suttas as part of a compound formed with the balancing quality of *pliancy.* In that compound, slightly different expressions are used, *ajjava-maddava,* explained in the commentary by *ujutā ca mudutā ca.* In these occurrences, however, *maddava* has not so much the psychological meaning of "pliancy of mind and concomitants," but should rather be understood in the ethical sense of "gentleness," which however is intimately connected with the psychological faculty of pliancy, as we have seen before (p. 73-74). This twofold concept of "straightness and gentleness" occurs, for example, at *AN* I 94 and is probably the source for its inclusion in the compendium-like *Saṅgīti Sutta* (*DN* III 213) and into the suttanta dyads of the *Dhammasaṅgaṇī* (§§ 1339–40). In the latter text the definitions of *ajjava-maddava* agree to a great extent with those of our two pairs, *ujukatā* and *mudutā,* in the same work (§§ 44, 45; 50, 51). Furthermore, these two terms (*ajjava-maddava*) appear at *AN* II 113 among the four qualities of a thoroughbred horse comparable to those of a noble monk, the other two qualities being swiftness (*java*) and patience (*khanti*). These latter two are likewise complementary qualities corresponding to the factors, agility and tranquillity. In the *Sutta-nipāta* we find (v. 250) "delighted in straightness linked to gentleness" (*ajjava-maddave rato*); in another passage (v. 292) they are given as qualities of the noble brahmins of old; in a third (v. 143; *Metta Sutta*) synonymous expressions appear among the qualities of an ideal monk:

Let him be capable and upright, truly upright,
Easily admonished, gentle and not haughty.
(Sakko ujū ca sūjū ca
Suvaco c'assa mudu anatimāni.)

The first part of this verse refers to firmness and strength of character, the second to gentleness. It furnishes an excellent though commonly overlooked example of how, also in the formation of character, the Buddha advocated a "middle path" on which seemingly contrary trends of character are harmonized into complementary qualities.

Pliancy and *workableness* of mind occur in the suttas very frequently and are usually mentioned together. We have already given two passages just above and shall quote only two more:

> With consciousness thus purified and cleansed, without blemish and stain, *pliant* and *workable*, steady and unshakable, he turns his mind to the extinction of the taints. (*MN* I 182, 347)

> Monks, there are five defilements of gold, owing to which gold is not *pliant*, not *workable*, impure, brittle, and cannot be well wrought.... Likewise, monks, there are these five defilements of the mind, owing to which the mind is not *pliant*, not *workable*, impure, brittle, and cannot concentrate well upon the extinction of the taints. What five? Sensual desire, ill will, rigidity and sloth, agitation and worry, doubt—these are the five defilements of the mind. (*SN* V 92–93)

Perhaps passages like this last were not only the source of the two pairs of pliancy and workableness but also inspired the composition of the entire group of six pairs of qualitative factors and their inclusion in the List of Dhammas. When the *Atthasālinī*, in its treatment of the six pairs, frequently refers to the five hindrances (*nīvaraṇa*), and when the subcommentary (see p. 74) uses the simile of gold to illustrate the consistency of mind necessary for the purpose of spiritual development, that too can be referred back to the passages just quoted.

The Purification of the Mind

Each wholesome thought, but especially the systematic culture of the mind (*bhāvanā*), is a process of elimination and refinement by which the gold of consciousness is gradually freed from blemishes and alien dross, and so brought to its true purity. As the Buddha says: "Monks, this mind is luminous (*pabhassaram*), but it is defiled by intrusive (*āgantukehi*) defilements. This mind is luminous, and it is freed from intrusive defilements" (*AN* I 10).[54]

Anything evil or unwholesome is to be seen as the "intrusion of a foreign element" that disturbs the mind's tranquillity with agitation; that prevents its agility with obstruction, its pliancy with hardening, its workableness with unbalance, and its proficiency with weakness; that deflects its uprightness. From that, it follows that the "six pairs of qualitative factors" belong in their totality only to *good* consciousness, and it is only as an inseparable group that they are included in the List of Dhammas.

It might be objected that there is keen-witted agility and adaptable pliancy also in a crook when thinking of some fraud. In such cases, however, these qualities are subservient to the greed or hate present in the same moment of consciousness and consequently they have a defiling effect on the mind of the evil-doer. Therefore they are not to be identified with the purifying qualities treated here. Besides, agitation (*uddhacca*), being a constant factor in each case of unwholesome consciousness, excludes the presence of tranquillity, and also the other five pairs would scarcely be complete in any unwholesome state of mind owing to the action of the specifically evil factors. Therefore the six pairs in their totality cannot enter unwholesome consciousness. But it is precisely the harmonious completeness (*sāmaggī*) of all the six pairs that gives them their peculiar character and makes them specific aspects of good consciousness. Only if all of them are present will they be able to exert their refining, tempering, and balancing influence on the structure of a good state of consciousness. Of course, they will not always be equally strong or perfectly balanced, but as universal good mental factors (*sobhana-sādhāraṇa*) they are present to a minimal degree in each state of good consciousness.

To contemplate the nature of these "six pairs of qualitative factors" is of great practical help to those who strive to purify the mind. In that contemplation, particular attention has to be given to the balancing of these factors. This has been briefly dealt with in the paragraph on their interrelation (p. 76-77). The sutta about the qualities of a thoroughbred horse (p. 78) and other passages quoted above show how the postulate of harmonization of character is inherent in the Buddhist scriptures, even when not expressly formulated in abstract terms. The balancing of the six pairs is complementary to the "harmonizing of the spiritual faculties" (*indriya-samatta*), the former referring to the formal or structural quality of consciousness, the latter to its actual functions.

In concluding this chapter, we would again stress that the most prominent feature in the Buddha's Teaching, that it is a middle path, refers not only to transcending extremes of thought and conduct but also to the formation and transformation of character.

11. The Helpers *(upakāraka, F51, 52)*

12. The Paired Combination *(yuganaddha, F53, 54)*

We suggest that the intention in including these two groups was to show that the mental factors present in any wholesome state of consciousness associated with knowledge offer the opportunity to practice different methods of spiritual development (*bhāvanā*), of which two examples are given here. They exemplify the *potentialities* of the wholesome state of consciousness, which belong as much to its dynamic structure as its actualities do.

The name "helpers" (*upakāraka*), given here to *mindfulness* (*sati*) and *mental clarity* (*sampajañña*), is derived from the *Atthasālinī*, which describes their role as that of helping (*upakāravasena*, p. 131).

These two factors refer to the practice of the Satipaṭṭhāna method. The *Mūlaṭīkā* makes a noteworthy comment, expressing well the character of Satipaṭṭhāna as the only and unique way (*ekāyano maggo*) (p. 92): "These two factors (*sati-sampajañña*) are 'helpers' (*upakāraka*) for any meditator, in any subject of meditation and at any time, because they remove obstacles and enhance spiritual development."

Calm (*samatha*) and *insight* (*vipassanā*) are the two complementary aspects of Buddhist mental culture. They also signify the different starting points for meditative practice chosen according to the disposition of the disciple, that is, having calm as vehicle (*samathayānika*) or having insight as vehicle (*vipassanāyānika*).[55] Lastly, they are the two main headings under which the traditional subjects of meditation may be classified. Though all these points may well be considered in this connection, in the *Atthasālinī* these two factors are viewed as phases of a particular method of meditation, called "the paired combination" (*yuganaddha*). This name was given to it because in that method periods of calm alternate with periods of insight. In the phase of calm, for example, the meditator attains the first jhāna, but rather than aim directly for the second jhāna he or she undertakes a period of insight (*vipassanā*) by contemplating the constituent factors of the jhāna as impermanent, suffering, and non-self. Then the meditator proceeds to the next jhāna, repeating the same process. This alternation of calm and insight is continued either through the whole sequence of absorptions or until one of the supramundane paths is thereby attained.

13. The Last Dyad *(piṭṭhi-duka, F55, 56)*

The two components of this group, *exertion* (*paggāha*) and *undistractedness* (*avikkhepa*), have been frequently mentioned already under various synonyms or aspects. There would have been no need to repeat them were it not in order to point out for the last time that these two factors are fundamental to spiritual progress. By joining them into a separate group it is emphasized that they should be not only strong singly but also well balanced, the one against the other. It is the harmony of the two spiritual faculties, energy and concentration—in other words, the middle path—that is stressed again here. This explanation is confirmed by the commentary (*Asl* 131): "These two terms are included in order to express the union of energy and concentration (*viriya-samādhi-yojanatthāya*)." The subcommentary adds: "With these two factors evenly joined (*samaṁ yuttā*) sluggishness as well as agitation are absent in every wholesome state of consciousness" (*DhsMṭ* 92).

It should, however, be noted that both factors can also appear in unwholesome consciousness where, in a different "environment," their kammic quality and their application are, of course, different.

14. The Supplementary Factors *(ye-vā-panaka, F57–65)*

The concluding passage in our text, called in the *Atthasālinī* "the addition" (*appaṇā*), runs as follows: "These phenomena, or whatsoever (*ye vā pana*) other conditionally arisen incorporeal phenomena there are at that time, are kammically wholesome." Thereby supplementations of the list are admitted, implying that the enumeration of mental factors given in it is not to be regarded as final. Such additions are in fact supplied by the commentaries (see *Asl* 131–32) and named the "or-whatsoever-factors" (*ye-vā-panakā*): an allusion to the above-quoted passage. The *Atthasālinī* says that these factors "are to be found in various passages of the suttas."

The nine supplementary factors that may appear in good consciousness are given in the table on p. 34. In addition to the first three (which are ethically variable), there are seven other factors that occur only in unwholesome consciousness.[56] All of them are incorporated into the condensed and systematized version of the List of Dhammas found in the *Visuddhimagga* and the *Abhidhammattha-saṅgaha*.[57] The first three factors—intention (*chanda*), decision (*adhimokkha*), and attention (*manasikāra*)—have rather important places in the later version of the list: "attention" belongs to the seven factors common to all consciousness (*sabbacittasādhāraṇa*); "decision" appears in seventy-eight of the eighty-nine types of consciousness; "intention" too is one of the most frequently occurring factors. All three of them are mentioned in that earlier list of *dhammas* given in the *Anupada Sutta* (see p. 49). In particular, the factor attention is very prominent in the suttas. It is mentioned as one of the three typical representatives of the aggregate of mental formations (*saṅkhārakkhandha*), for example, in the *Sammādiṭṭhi Sutta* (*MN* No. 9),[58] which was likewise delivered by that first early Ābhidhammika, the Venerable Sāriputta: "Feeling, perception, volition, sense-contact, and attention—these, brethren, are called mind (*nāma*)" (*MN* I 53). Also in post-canonical books, attention is mentioned, for example, in the *Milindapañha* and the *Nettippakaraṇa*. In view of all these facts it is surprising that attention at least was not included in our list. In view of the prominent place occupied by this mental factor in the Pāli suttas, oversight has to be excluded and intentional omission to be assumed, also in the case of the other supplementary factors. But we have not been able to form any convincing opinion about the reasons for this. Obviously, in the first composition of the list these factors must have been thought supernumerary, but were again admitted by the later redactors.

It may be of interest to compare in this respect the lists of *dhammas* composed by the later Buddhist schools. The lists of both the Hīnayānist Sarvāstivādins and the Mahāyānist Vijñānavādins include the three neutral supplementary factors (intention, decision, and attention) and the unwholesome ones. In the list of the Sarvāstivādins the three neutral ones are found among the "factors common to all consciousness" (called there *mahābhūmika*), and in that respect they differ from the Theravādins, who allow only attention in that group. The Vijñānavādins, agreeing in that point with the Pāli list, relegated decision and intention to a group of inconstant neutral factors.

This concludes the treatment of the single groups forming the List of Dhammas in the *Dhammasaṅgaṇī*.

15. Gradations of Intensity among Parallel Factors

Having dealt with the single groups among which the various parallel factors appear, we may now point to some facts that show how the multiple enumeration of apparently identical factors serves to express a difference of intensity or quality. As far as we know, these facts, as registered in the following table, have so far not been noticed. There is no mention of them in the *Atthasālinī* or the *Mūlaṭīkā*, nor apparently in any later literature.

Let us take a set of parallel factors, for instance: mental one-pointedness, faculty of concentration, power of concentration, path factor of concentration (right and wrong), calm, and undistractedness. Now if we look for their definition as given after each principal paragraph in the *Dhammasaṅgaṇī*, we find that these definitions are almost identical for all the parallel factors, in nearly every case.[59] There are only the following differences: in unwholesome consciousness right concentration is replaced by wrong concentration in the text of the definition itself, not only in the enumeration of factors. In supramundane consciousness (*lokuttara*), the concentration factor of enlightenment (*samādhi-sambojjhaṅga*) is added. These divergences do not refer to differing intensity. But one case of a varying definition does so, and it is unique in this respect among all other factors: in the case of seventeen weak types of consciousness (see the table below), the definition of mental one-pointedness stops with the first term "stability" (*ṭhiti*). If we were to judge only by comparing the definitions, the last-mentioned single exception would only prove the general rule that no differentiation of intensity is intended among the parallel factors.

But the definitions in the *Dhammasaṅgaṇī* are not a sufficient criterion since they are rather rigid formulas that undergo only those very few changes mentioned above. Owing to their rigidity even some minor inconsistencies between the definitions and the structure of the respective states of consciousness do occur, as we shall see later on. Therefore, to decide the question of degrees of intensity among parallel factors, we shall also have to examine and compare the actual inclusion or omission of those quasi-synonyms in the single states of consciousness. There is only one set of parallel factors, beginning with mental one-pointedness (see above), which allows such a survey of the whole field of consciousness (that is, wholesome, unwholesome, kamma-resultant, and functional).

We supplement it by one variation occurring in the case of energy (*viriya*) and tabulate the results in the accompanying table:[60]

Type of Consciousness		Parallel Factors	
Tab. No.	*Description*	*Present*	*Absent*
32	Unwholesome, associated with doubt	Mental one-pointedness (defined only by "stability")	Concentration as faculty, power, path factor, calm, undistractedness
34-38, 50-54	5-sense-consciousness	"	"
39, 55	Receiving of sense object; resultant	"	"
40	Investigating and registering (joyful)	"	"
41, 56	Investigating and registering (indifferent), rebirth & death-consciousness, *bhavaṅga*	"	"
70	Functional: 5-door adverting	"	"
71	Functional: mind-door adverting; determining	(*a*) One-pointedness (complete definition); concentration as faculty	Concentration as power, and path factor; undistractedness
		(*b*) faculty of energy	Power of energy; effort as path factor; exertion
72	Functional: arahant's smiling consciousness	"	"

This tabulation permits the following conclusions:

1. Among the set of parallel factors denoting "concentration," three degrees of intensity are noticeable: (*a*) mental one-pointedness, standing alone, its definition limited to "stability," signifying the weakest degree of concentration (seventeen types: 32, 34–38, 50–54, 39, 55, 40, 41, 56, 70); (*b*) mental one-pointedness joined only by the faculty of concentration, but with the definition having the complete number of terms (two types: 71, 72); (*c*) mental one-pointedness with the entire set of parallel factors, as in all other classes of consciousness.

2. In the case of energy (*viriya*), there are only two gradations of intensity: There is no weaker degree of it than the *indriya*-aspect; for energy is not a constant factor like mental one-pointedness. This implies that energy has always a certain controlling influence, but that mental one-pointedness in its weakest state has not. The two gradations are (*a*) the faculty of energy standing alone; and (*b*) the faculty of energy with the entire set of parallel factors.

3. According to the use of the two terms in the Abhidhamma, the faculty-aspect of a quality may be present without the power-aspect. This applies, however, only in the case of the two ethically neutral faculties, concentration and energy, and occurs only in two types of consciousness (71, 72). It implies that the three exclusively wholesome faculties (faith, mindfulness, and wisdom) always appear together with their power-aspect.

4. The powers, path factors, calm, exertion, and undistractedness occur exclusively (*a*) in kammic consciousness (wholesome and unwholesome); (*b*) in those "strong" kamma-resultant (*vipāka*) and functional (*kiriya*) states that exactly correspond in their structure to the eight wholesome kammic types. These are the eight main resultants of wholesome kamma (*mahāvipāka*), and the eight functional states occurring only in the case of the arahant (*kiriyajavana*).

If the facts tabulated above, and especially our conclusions 1–3, had been noticed, they would certainly have been mentioned in the *Atthasālinī*. These facts, indeed, would have necessitated definitions more differentiated than those given in the *Atthasālinī*, for mental one-pointedness and for the faculties and powers of concentration and energy, taking into consideration the above gradation of intensity.

The instances of the separate occurrence of the faculties without the powers cannot be explained as an unintentional omission of the power-aspect by scribes, because we are here able to check the correctness of the text by reference to the Summary Section in the *Dhammasaṅgaṇī*, where the number of faculties, powers, etc., is always listed.

The definitions in the *Dhammasaṅgaṇī* include the different aspects, that is, the parallels of the respective factors. But on comparing them with their actual appearance in the given states of consciousness in the list, some minor inconsistencies between the definition and the list are found: in nos. 71, 72 in the table the definition of mental one-pointedness includes the faculty as well as the power of concentration, but the latter is not present in these types as a separate factor, as the table shows; there is a corresponding divergence in the case of the faculty, and the power, of energy. This illustrates our previous remark that the definitions cannot be used as the sole criterion for determining the quality of the respective factor.

The facts pointed out in this chapter support our contention that the multiple enumeration of mental factors in the List of Dhammas is not a mere dispensable elaboration, and that each parallel factor has a more or less important and varying individual significance.

16. Concluding Remarks

These investigations arose out of the question: Why is the List of Dhammas in the *Dhammasaṅgaṇī* filled out with so many quasi-synonyms, and what purpose do these synonyms serve? This poses a further question: Are there any reasons for still making use of these original and somewhat cumbersome lists in view of their handy abbreviation and systematization in the *Visuddhimagga* and the *Abhidhammattha-saṅgaha*? The answer to these questions may now be given by summarizing our investigations as follows: The enumeration of parallel factors has an individual and a relational significance; that is, it concerns, first, the particular nature of the single factor itself and, second, the various connections or relations of that factor.

Individual Significance

1. The multiple enumeration illustrates the *different functions and ways of application of a single quality.* This is the only explanation given in the *Atthasālinī* (see p. 37-38); all the others that follow are inferences and conclusions drawn from a close examination of the sources.

From the point of view of theoretical and abstract psychology the inclusion of mere functions and aspects may appear superfluous or even a proof of "loose thinking" and "unscientific procedure." But for the ultimately practical—that is, spiritual—purposes of Buddhist psychology it is essential to stress the several important functions and applications of qualities. Even in the field of theory the more advanced psychology of our own time recognizes this procedure, for instance in those succinctly coined words of James Ward chosen as the epigraph for our chapter 4: "A difference in aspects is a difference in things." This is a remarkable approach to the dynamic psychology of the Abhidhamma.

2. The multiple enumeration makes it possible to register varying *degrees of intensity* in the actual functioning of a single factor (see the previous section).

Relational Significance

1. The multiple enumeration, together with the arrangement in groups, shows the *internal relations* of a factor, that is, its varied connections with other factors present in the same moment of consciousness. These internal relations include such common functions as the controlling function of the faculties; such common purposes as the liberating purpose of the path factors. This implies two postulates of great practical importance: in a state of consciousness a multitude of factors cooperate to achieve a common purpose, whether that be of a worldly or spiritual nature; individual qualities that are often wrongly considered to be opposed are actually complementary and thus should not be pitted against each other but brought into harmony.

2. The multiple enumeration and arrangement in groups suggests, by implication, that we pursue and investigate the *external relations* of factors and groups, that is, the connection of a given moment of consciousness with past and future ones. This includes the close investigation of the conditioned as well as the conditioning nature of a single state of consciousness—a task to be undertaken with the terminological tools provided in the *Paṭṭhāna.* The conditioned nature of a phenomenon points to its external relations with the past, while the conditioning aspect draws attention to its external relations with the future. But it should be kept in mind that in both cases internal relations as well are involved, that is, conditions obtaining in the present (support, mutuality, etc.).

3. The multiple enumeration and the arrangement in groups can help us to find the *potentialities* of a factor or a group or an entire state of consciousness. Properly, this point is included in that last mentioned, namely, in the external relations with the future. But for the sake of emphasis it is mentioned here separately. *In order to do full justice to the dynamic nature of consciousness, not only its actual functions but also its inherent potentialities have to be considered.* Particularly in Buddhist psychology, which is, or should be, completely subservient to the practical task of spiritual development, it is imperative to look out for the "seeds" embedded in a given situation, that is, to observe whether a state of mind possesses the potentiality for good and better or for bad and worse. To give an example: an *actual* but limited control wielded by the spiritual faculties implies the *potential* increase of that control; an *actual* but weak liberating influence exercised by the path factors implies the *potential* strengthening of their liberating effect. Besides, "potentiality" sometimes means that the particular state of mind *gravitates* in the direction indicated by the potentiality. So by giving due attention to the potentiality one can foresee future developments and either assist or counter them in time.

These and other considerations will show that the elaborate original version of the List of Dhammas as given in the *Dhammasaṅgaṇī* is not in the least rendered superfluous by its condensation in the *Visuddhimagga* and its systematization in the

Abhidhammattha-saṅgaha. Of course, the reverse is not suggested here, namely, that those later versions should be disregarded in favor of the original. Their handiness is a great advantage, and in many cases it suffices to use them instead of the elaborate original. These later versions have also made the valuable contribution of incorporating the supplementary factors. On the other hand, it has to be regretted that, to our knowledge, the use of the original canonical list has been completely superseded in later Abhidhamma literature by the condensed version, and thus several important and fruitful lines of thought implied in the particular features of the original version, or derivable from it, have been left undeveloped. There is, for example, the arrangement of the factors in groups, which has been emphasized in these pages. Having been almost obliterated in the later condensed versions of the list, that arrangement should be restored to its rightful place. The arrangement in groups is not only relevant to the details of the subject matter but is also of great general and methodological importance. For the fact of grouping has introduced a synthetical or relational element into the preeminently analytical *Dhammasaṅgaṇī.* It serves as a corrective and as a complementary principle. This is required because—as already stated at the beginning of this treatise—a composite thing is not yet sufficiently described if only its single parts are enumerated separately without due regard to their internal and external relations. If wheels, axle, carriage, etc., are placed separately on the ground, they cannot yet be called a cart. Only if parts of a whole are shown in their purposeful combination, if not in their actual operation, are we dealing with realities and not with artificial abstractions. In our analytical endeavors we should never forget the fundamental, though temporal, "unity of experience," that is, the internal relations, and the greater "unity of the continuous flux," that is, the external relations. This should always be remembered by those engaged in studying the Abhidhamma.

Here only a modest beginning has been made in the investigation of the ingenious combination of the analytical and synthetical methods in Buddhist philosophy. These pages appeal for research in that direction to continue. For those who want to do this work thoroughly, tremendous preliminary labor is waiting, namely, to convert the abstract formulas of the *Paṭṭhāna* into terms of actuality giving concrete examples in a sufficiently comprehensive selection for the relations treated there.

V

The Problem of Time

1. Time and Consciousness

The formula of the *Dhammasaṅgaṇī*—"At a time when..." (see p. 31)—implies a close connection between time and consciousness, which in a verse quoted in the *Atthasālinī* (p. 57) is described as a mutual relationship:

By time the Sage described the mind
And by the mind described the time,
In order to show, by such definition,
The phenomena there arranged in classes.

(Samaye niddisi cittaṁ cittena samayaṁ muni
niyametvāna dīpetuṁ dhamme tattha pabhedato.)

The state of consciousness classified in the first part of the schematic sentence of the *Dhammasaṅgaṇī* is, in its existence, *limited* as well as *described* by time. The duration of that mind-defining time period is circumscribed by the simultaneity of the mental factors enumerated in the second part of the sentence ("... at that time there are sense-contact ..."). In other words, a state of consciousness lasts as long as the combination of its single factors. This represents the *limitation* of consciousness by time. Its *description* too is only possible by reference to time, namely, to the temporary simultaneity of the single factors. Conversely, these mental factors—in other words, the internal relations—for their part determine the time by furnishing the measure of the time unit, which consists only in the duration of that temporary combination of factors. The conclusion to be drawn from this mutual relation between time and consciousness may be formulated in the words of Bertrand Russell: "...we cannot give what may be called *absolute* dates, but only dates determined by events. We cannot point to a time itself, but only to some event occurring at that time."[61] The commentator expresses the same idea when, in explaining the word *samaya* (rendered in our translation by "time"), he says: "Chronological time, denoted by reference to this or that (event), is merely a conventional expression... Since it has no existence in itself (i.e., cannot be found in reality) one has to understand it as a mere concept."[62]

According to the commentary (*Asl* 57–61), the term *samaya* in the sentence from the *Dhammasaṅgaṇī* expresses five meanings:

1. The first is *chronological time* (*kālo = pavattikālo*, "duration"), which we have just discussed.

2. *Concurrence* (*samavāya*) of circumstances, that is, the completeness of conditions (*paccaya-sāmaggī*) necessary for the occurrence of the particular state of consciousness. For example, visual organ, visual object, light, attention, etc., are required for the arising of visual consciousness. This meaning of *samaya* relates the given moment of consciousness to the present, that is, to coexisting conditions.

3. *Condition* (*hetu*), that is, the combination of those modes of conditionality that are operative in the particular case. For example, for visual consciousness, the visual organ and object are conditions by way of prenascence (*purejāta-paccaya*); visual consciousness (*dassana*) is related to the preceding perceptual phase of incipient attention (*āvajjana*, "mental adverting") by way of immediate contiguity (*samanantara-paccaya*); for the subsequent phases of that visual experience the visual consciousness is a condition by way of inducement (*upanissaya*), object (*ārammaṇa*), predominance (*adhipati*), etc. This meaning of *samaya* relates to all three divisions of time. The future is likewise included because every state of consciousness is not only conditioned but is itself a condition for subsequent states.

4. The right *moment* (*khaṇa*) refers only to wholesome consciousness. It means: the right occasion for additional wholesome activity for which the present moment of wholesome consciousness is capable of being an inducement, support, and starting point. Whether this "right moment" is properly utilized depends on the awareness of that opportunity; if such awareness is absent the potentialities inherent in the moment will be lost. This connotation of *samaya* refers only to the future.

5. *Aggregation* (*samūha*), that is, the momentary union of the single components of consciousness, the "constellation" that determines the psychological time, just as the constellation of *samaya* refers only to the present.

The simultaneity of mental factors referred to above is not a static juxtaposition of self-contained units as in a mosaic. Their simultaneity results rather from different processes of psychic movements meeting temporarily in the constellation of the present moment, partly overlapping each other but without achieving complete congruity, just as in nature there are also no truly congruent triangles.

A glance into the "antecedents" and the subsequent "life story" of the factors of a single moment of consciousness will show us: (1) that the simultaneity of these factors has to be conceived as something fluid and not static; (2) that simultaneous factors, insofar as they are variable (nonconstant), meet each other at quite different stages of their own "life history": some factors might already have been parts of preceding moments but are disappearing with the dissolution of the present one; some arise only now and recur in future moments; and again, the lifetime of others may be limited to this moment only. Such a differentiation is certainly significant, just as it makes a difference whether we meet with certain people or ideas in youth, maturity, or old age.

The fact that parts of other moments of consciousness may, as it were, spread over the present moment or extend beyond it makes for an intricate interlacing and a close organic continuity in the world of mental phenomena. There are no "empty spaces," no disconnected events in the universe of the mind, though the connection may often be very loose and remote. Even if a psychic event breaks in quite unexpectedly, it does not arise from nothingness but is related to a perhaps distant past, the gap being bridged by subconscious mental processes. Here we meet again the "third dimension" of mind—its "depth" with regard to time, already referred to (p. 29).

A minimum of psychic continuity is always given by the seven "factors common to all consciousness" (see note 40) But we also have to keep in mind the element of diversity in those seven factors. In their repeated occurrence and concrete manifestations, far from being identical, they are actually highly varied. They are "common" factors only as concepts abstracted for the purpose of methodical exposition, though they do possess enough (relative) identity to maintain the continuity in the mental process. Also, with regard to the already mentioned connection of an unexpected event with its conditions in the past, we must not forget the element of diversity. Taking this into account we spoke intentionally of the event as being *related* to a past event, not as being caused by it, which happens only in certain cases. Otherwise we should land in complete determinism, which results in a static view of the world. Though, strictly speaking, there are no completely new events in the material and mental universe, there are also no fully identical repetitions. The truth is in between, that is, in the middle path of dependent origination: "Both these two extremes the Perfect One has avoided and has shown the middle doctrine (*majjhena dhammaṁ*), which says: "With ignorance as condition the kamma-formations come to be" (*SN* II 20). That is to say, the middle path of the Buddha appears here as the law of conditionality—as the fact of correlation, which is what is really implied when we speak, somewhat vaguely, of continuity. It is, in fact, the energy inherent in the conditions (*paccaya-satti*) that creates what is called continuity or a continuum.

To effect continuity is a prominent function of consciousness, and this was already recognized in the *Atthasālinī*. Among the traditional categories of definition, the manifestation (*paccupaṭṭhāna*) of consciousness is called "connecting" (*sandahana*), which is explained as follows: "Consciousness presents itself as 'connecting,' because when any later state of consciousness arises, it does so by immediately succeeding the preceding state; that is why 'connecting' is its manifestation."[63]

This implies that each state of consciousness is "open" to the past as well as to the future: it has "depth" in time. Though a moment of consciousness has no rigid boundaries, it nevertheless does not lack individuality—in the same way as there will be a characteristic blend of colors where several multicolored beams of light intersect; but its shade will change at once if even one of these beams of light moves away or varies its intensity. Likewise, when a change of direction or intensity occurs in the components of consciousness, the "color" of the subsequent mental state will be different. Apart from the divergent past and future "life story" of the single components of consciousness, also in the point of their intersection, that is, in the given moment of consciousness, there is no motionless stability or self-identity. A single moment too passes through the three phases: (1) the arising (*uppāda*) or the nascent state; (2) the (relative) stability (*ṭhiti*) or state of continuation, which may be understood as the culmination point of the respective process or as the point of the closest contact in the temporary combination of mental factors; (3) the gradual dissolution (*bhaṅga*) of that combination. In other words, these three phases represent the approaching and departing movement in the mutual relationship of the mental concomitants. This corresponds to the changes occurring in that greater temporary combination called "personality," and in the still greater one of society, where a similar rhythm may be observed. We spoke of this previously as the alternating process of assimilation and dissimilation.

Here in this context our purpose is merely to explain the first statement of the commentarial stanza quoted above: "By time the Sage described the mind..." We found that this statement has a twofold meaning: firstly, a moment of consciousness is limited in its duration by the simultaneity of its concomitants, and only by that simultaneity of factors can a description of it be given; secondly, a moment of consciousness, in its full significance, with all its implications, can be explained only in terms of time, and by referring to all three divisions of time—to the past, present, and future. Because of the conditioned nature of consciousness, no present mental state is self-explanatory.

The second line of the stanza says: "And by the mind [he] described the time." This means that the *time* mentioned in the second part of the sentence (i.e., the duration of the mental factors in their momentary combination) is referred to, and thereby described by, the state of *consciousness* as classified in the first part of the sentence. Here, time is "denoted by reference to" consciousness (*upādāya paññatto kālo*). But quite apart from the denotation and description of a particular time period in terms of consciousness, time in general can be conceived only as the conscious experience of it. This subjective—or better, psychological—character of time becomes particularly distinct when time seems to pass either very slowly or very quickly: slowly in a mental state of dullness or expectancy, quickly in interesting activity or mental absorption. Other examples of the decisive influence of the psychological factor in the experience of time are the contraction of time in dreams as well as in the flashlike retrospect of one's entire life when faced with death. It is also evident that there will be a different time experience and time value in the lives of an ephemerid, a dog, a man, and a two-hundred-year-old tortoise. To an insect living but a single day, the morning, noon, and evening of that day will have the same significance as childhood, maturity, and old age have for us. Each creature, at the end of its life span, will feel that it has lived a full life, irrespective of the number of the hypothetical "objective" time units. William James says: "We have every reason to think that creatures may possibly differ enormously in the amount of duration which they intuitively feel..."[64] We may tentatively say that time value or time experience depends on the intensity of consciousness and on the life span, the first being the more "subjective" and the other the more "objective" factor. This shows again the interweaving of these two forces—subjectification and objectification—in each aspect of life, which we earlier illustrated by the internal and external relations present in each moment of consciousness.

These examples of the psychological character of time suggest that there exist different planes of time corresponding to different levels of consciousness. A few provisional remarks about this are given in the next section.

2. Planes of Time

It is now held that each series of events has its own time order, and it is difficult to relate the one to the other since there is no common standard time.

—Sir James Jeans, *The Mysterious Universe*

From what was said in the last chapter it seems that the Buddhist teaching of the relativity of time is not limited merely to the statement that time is a relational concept, related to, and inseparable from, the events occurring in it. By inference we may assume that Buddhist philosophy also acknowledges different *planes* of time, though they are not mentioned as such. This puts the relativity of time on a still wider basis.

Any phase or aspect of any life process has the inherent potentiality of an increase or decrease in the scale of its varying intensity, extending far beyond the horizon of the particular point of observation. Science has shown that there are sound and light waves beyond our perceptual range ascertainable by deduction or by experiment with an apparatus more sensitive than our human sensorium. In the same way we need not suppose that time is limited to the radius of the human time experience and that there is no increase or decrease in its intensity. There are certainly time planes below and above the range of average human consciousness, which may likewise be either inferred by deductive methods or actually experienced in the "experimental situation" of meditative practice, in which the range and sensitivity of average consciousness may be greatly expanded.

In Pāli Buddhist literature we have found only two express references to different time planes, and these are extreme cases below and above the average time experience. The fact that they are extreme cases might be accidental and attributable to our still uncompleted survey of the scriptures from that point of view; or it can be explained by the fact that the differentiation of time levels is more evident in such extreme cases and cannot be neglected when the respective phenomena are investigated. These two cases are: (1) matter, and (2) the meditative attainment of cessation (*nirodha-samāpatti*).

Matter. In the postcanonical Abhidhamma literature it is said that the duration of a material phenomenon is equal to sixteen moments of consciousness. In other words, one material time unit equals sixteen mental time units of average human consciousness. The number "sixteen" should not be taken as a definite time measure, the less so since the unit of one moment of consciousness is metaphorically defined as "the billionth part of a flash of lightning." It is only the ratio of 1:16—a comparative relation—that is expressed here. In the same way, a complete process of sense perception (*pañcadvāravīthi*) has been hypothetically determined as lasting sixteen moments,[65] in order to fix the proportional duration of the single phases of that process; for example, impulsion (*javana*) occupies seven of these sixteen. The relative duration of a material unit was determined as equalling that of a complete perceptual process, that is, sixteen moments. The choice of the number "sixteen" may have been influenced by the fact that in India this number was (and is) a very popular measuring unit of space, time, etc., often used metaphorically.[66] A Westerner with his decimal system might have chosen "ten" as a starting point for distributing proportional values.

By the ratio 1:16 an estimate of the relative velocity of corporeal and mental processes is given—the former being considerably slower than the latter. The commentary to the *Vibhaṅga* says: "In corporeal things change is difficult and cessation slow; in mental things change is easy and cessation quick."[67]

To circumscribe in that way the time rhythm of corporeal things in terms of consciousness is justified (1) by the second principle laid down in the commentarial stanza, "And by the mind [he] described the time"; and (2) by the close connection between time and consciousness corresponding to the connection between space and matter. But there is yet a third point that is important to remember when material processes are related to or explained by mental ones: it is a fundamental idea of Buddhist philosophy that matter cannot exist without a kammic consciousness desiring life in a material world: "If, Ānanda, there were no kamma maturing in the sensuous sphere, could sensuous existence (*kāmabhava*) appear?"—"Surely not, Lord" (*AN* I 223).

Of course, this must not be taken to imply an idealistic conclusion; for mind, like all component things, is a conditioned phenomenon and cannot be regarded as a sole cause, be it of matter or of anything else. But, avoiding the extreme beliefs in primacy of matter or primacy of mind, we can say that both matter and mind are manifestations of kammic energy at varying distances from the generative source of that energy. We may also express it thus: that around the center of generative kammic energy several peripheral circles revolve. Closest to the center we have to imagine the kamma-results proper (*vipāka*), which are only mental states. Next comes the circle of such matter as is directly produced by kamma (*kammaja-* or *kamma-samuṭṭhāna-rūpa*), which is only one division of matter. After that come kinds of matter produced by consciousness (*cittasamuṭṭhāna*), by food (*āhārasamuṭṭhāna*), and by such physical influences as temperature (*utusamuṭṭhāna*).[68] The latter, too, though most distant from the center, must be assumed to be still connected with the kammic force.

Though the rhythm of matter is so much slower than that of mind, the lifetime of a single material unit is as little within the range of our direct perception as that of a mental unit. Nevertheless, it is owing to that increase in duration that such continua of inorganic matter as are directly perceptible produce the impression of relative constancy. And this impression of the constancy of matter, linked with the innate human longing for permanency, not only allows the poet's mind, so sensitive to the fleetingness of short-lived things, to find a spell of soothing rest in the contemplation of the "eternal hills," but is also responsible for theories about the primacy of matter and for belief in an objective and abiding material world. The probability that this our earth may still exist long after all human, animal, and plant life has vanished is different only in degree, but not in essence, from such evident facts as that the work may outlive the worker, an effect its cause, etc.

The Attainment of Cessation. While matter exists on a time level—or better, changes in a time rhythm—slower than that of mind, and comparable to the infrared end of the spectrum, there are also vibrations corresponding to the ultraviolet rays, which are so completely beyond the range of average human consciousness that, in the Buddhist psychology of meditative experience, they are only spoken of in terms of negation and exclusion similar to Nibbāna. We refer here to the meditative attainment of cessation (*nirodha-samāpatti*), a term that signifies the temporary cessation of perception and feeling (*saññā-vedayita-nirodha*). There are also gradual transitions to that highly abstract ultraconscious state, just as there are between any two points in the round of *saṁsāra*. These transitions are the four formless absorptions (*āruppa*). Here the rate of mental vibrations is already so intensified as to suspend contact with the world of matter and its special time rhythm. The suspension can take place either in the brief periods of meditative absorption in the case of a human meditator, or in an inconceivably long life span in the case of a rebirth in the formless worlds (*arūpaloka*).

In this context it is worth noting that what is now an exceptional meditative experience may, if the affinity with that experience is sufficiently strong, become the normal status in a new existence. Any peripheral events may become the center, and exceptions the rule, of a new life in a higher or lower sphere. The territories of the saṁsāric spheres have fluid boundaries. "Neighboring" spheres may widely overlap. Human life, for example, is in certain respects regulated by laws pertaining to the realm of matter and to the vegetable and animal kingdoms. The human mind requires the regular tidal movement between the peak of its strenuous activity during the day and its subsidence into the subconsciousness of sleep. The interpenetration with higher regions, surpassing average human consciousness, is much less extensive and much rarer. There are, indeed, some rare contacts with the realm of higher spirituality and intensified consciousness: in meditation, religious inspiration, artistic intuition, etc.; but they are followed only too quickly by a relapse into the relative dullness of everyday consciousness.

So there is, first, an actual and regular interpenetration with lower spheres, including their different time levels; and, second, there are the potential or rare contacts with the higher planes of existence and time, which may extend up to the four formless absorptions. The last of them (which may be followed by the attainment of cessation) is called *nevasaññā-nāsaññāyatana*, "the sphere of neither-perception-nor-nonperception" ("the ultimate limit of perception," Anagārika Govinda). The twofold negation in the name of this meditative state has to be understood as referring not only to the function of perception but to all components of consciousness. Here consciousness has reached such a degree of refinement that even the name "consciousness" is no longer quite appropriate and is retained only because there is still a residuum of sublime mental activities directed to the most abstract and sublime object imaginable: the previously obtained experience of the sphere of nothingness, which is the preceding stage of attainment. Here the tension between the subject and object is naturally so exceedingly low that all that we call consciousness and time is on the point of vanishing completely. Consciousness, in fact, means to be aware of an object, and "time experience" means being aware of the relative movements of the subjective and objective aspects of a perceptual process.

The borderline of consciousness and time, reached in that fourth formless absorption, is transcended by the *attainment of cessation.* This is trenchantly expressed by the exclusion of that meditative state (1) from the normal time order of subsequent mental states, and (2) from the systematization of all "things" in the *Dhammasaṅgaṇī.*

The first point, exclusion from the normal time order, is stated in the *Paṭṭhāna* (*Pañha-vāra* §§4, 5) in the following way: "After emergence from the attainment of cessation, the (previously obtained) wholesome state of the sphere of neither-perception-nor-nonperception is a condition for the attainment of fruition (of the nonreturner or arahant), by way of proximity or contiguity condition (*anantara-* or *samanantara-paccaya*)." When the time relation of the two other states is said to be one of immediate succession, this means that the intervening attainment of cessation is not counted. The obvious conclusion to draw is that the state of cessation is assumed to take place on quite a different time level. This is emphasized by the statement that from the view of the human time rhythm, the attainment of cessation may last for seven days.

As to the second point, the exclusion from the "Enumeration of Things" (*Dhammasaṅgaṇī*), we read in the *Atthasālinī* (p. 346): "It has been pointed out that in this triad (of wholesome, unwholesome, and indeterminate phenomena) the following states do not obtain: the three characteristics, the three concepts, the space obtained after the removal of the *kasiṇa*, empty space, the object of the consciousness of the sphere of nothingness (that is, the void aspect of the consciousness of infinite space), and the *attainment of cessation*."

The *Mūlaṭīkā* remarks that all these are excluded because they are not "real things" (*sabhāvadhamma*): "There is no real thing not contained in the triad of the wholesome, etc." (p. 160). Furthermore, the *Visuddhimagga* remarks (p. 709): "The attainment of cessation can neither be said to be conditioned nor unconditioned (*saṅkhata-asaṅkhata*), neither mundane nor supramundane (*lokiya-lokuttara*). Why not? Because it does not exist as a real entity (*sabhāvato natthitāya*). But because it has been entered into by the meditator, it is called 'produced' (*nipphanna*) and not 'unproduced' (*anipphanna*)."

When, in the above passage, the quality of a "real thing" is denied to the attainment of cessation, this certainly does not mean that this state is "unreal" in the sense of a hallucination or a figment of the imagination. We should therefore better speak of it as being "differently real" because all the data of our experience of reality and even of the most sublime states of absorption are absent in that state. In the same way, Nibbāna may be said to have no "existence" in terms of the *khandha*-world, but by denying its reality we would fall into the error of annihilationism (*ucchedadiṭṭhi*).

In this context our aim was only to put on record that Buddhist psychology of meditative experience knows of a time level that leaves our own so far behind that it can only be spoken of by a paradoxical statement, namely, by its assignation to, as well as the annulment of, seven days of our own calendar.

3. The Concept of the Present in the Abhidhamma

The Depth Dimension of Time

We have observed earlier (pp. 29-30) how Buddhist philosophy does not stop short at the rigid and "two-dimensional" concept of time, and particularly of the present, resulting from analysis.

Through its philosophy of relations involving a synthetical method, the Abhidhamma adds the third dimension of "depth in time." When subjected to analytical treatment alone, the present tends to become an insignificant point of intersection between past and future with a most elusive and even illusory nature. But when the depth dimension is added it becomes charged with energies deriving from the past and with a significance extending to the future—both in varying degrees, starting from very weak connections up to a definitely determined course, which is, however, limited to very few cases.[69] To express this dynamic view of time, special terms were required beyond the conventional and therefore too static concepts of past, present, and future. We proffer the opinion that it was for this purpose that the "triad of things arisen, not arisen, and bound to arise" (*uppannā, anuppannā, uppādino dhammā*) was included in the *Dhammasaṅgaṇī* (at §§1035–37) and that the commentarial four categories of *uppannā* were formed, which will be dealt with later.

But the "triad of things arisen" was not intended to supersede the "triad of things past, present, and future" which remains at *Dhs* §§1038–40. The latter has an importance of its own in the much more frequent cases when it is necessary to distinguish between the three periods of time and the objects existing in them. Also, as a corrective against the opposite extreme, this triad is required in order to insist on the (relative) differentiation of the three periods of time and to counter the tendency to obliterate them completely. This tendency (as well as its opposite) appears again and again in the history of philosophy, and the following emphatic words of the Buddha may well have been directed against similar contemporary ideas:

> Monks, there are three unconfounded appellations, expressions, and designations. Unconfounded before, they are now unconfounded and cannot be confounded; they are not rejected by wise ascetics and brahmins. Which are these three? For such corporeality (feeling, etc.) that is past, gone, and changed, "It has been," is here the (right) statement, the usage, the designation. The statement "It is" does not apply to it, the statement "It will be" does not apply to it. (*SN* III 71–72)[70]

Within the Buddhist fold the philosophical trend to obliterate the distinction between the three periods of time came very much to the fore among the Sarvāstivādins, who maintained that *dharmas* (conceived as the ultimate unchangeable elements of existence) persist through all three periods of time, which have only conventional validity, and that things appearing in these three time periods have only phenomenal existence. These ideas obviously contradict two basic conceptions of Buddhist doctrine, namely, impermanence and insubstantiality. In view of such consequences it is therefore imperative not to forget the relative differentiation of time manifested in the fact of change or impermanence. Following the principle of the twofold method, we stress this complementary aspect just here before proceeding to deal with the other, more neglected aspect of the relations between the three periods of time, in which partial interpenetration is prominent.

Before dealing with the term *uppanna*, which is particularly relevant in that connection, we shall mention briefly the three divisions of the term *paccuppanna*, "present."[71] These three kinds of the "present" are given in an order of increasing duration:

1. The "momentary present" (*khaṇa-paccuppanna*), extending only over the three phases of a single moment of consciousness: this is to be regarded as the present in the strict sense, though not actually perceptible.

2. The "serial present" (*santati-paccuppanna*), comprising a series or continuum (*santati*) of moments. The *Atthasālinī* records the definitions made by two schools. The first (the reciters of the *Majjhima Nikāya*) says that it lasts for one or two continua (*santati*), which are defined by examples such as the time required for things to become visible after an abrupt change from daylight to a dark room or conversely. The second school of thought (the reciters of the *Saṁyutta Nikāya*) distinguishes material and mental continua. The former are explained by the aforementioned and other examples, the latter by the duration of two or three processes of impulsion (*javanavīthi*), that is, by two or three processes of a complete perception, each lasting sixteen moments. We should hesitate to ascribe actual perceptibility to a duration of two or three processes, though on the other hand

the earlier examples imply a duration somewhat too long to convey the idea of "present." Still we must suppose that the second division, the "serial present," is intended to refer to the actual experience of a "now."

3. The third division stands apart: it is the present with reference to the present life term or present birth process (*addhā-paccuppanna*).

The Fourfold Meaning of Arisen

We now turn to the term *uppanna*, "arisen," for which a fourfold division is given:[72]

1. *Vattamān'uppanna*, that is, presently or actually arisen. *Uppanna*, being grammatically a past participle, can also be taken here in the meaning of a "present tense" for which *vattamāna* is the grammatical term. It is identical with the "momentary present" (*khaṇa-paccuppanna*; see above).

2. *Bhūtāpagat'uppanna*, that is, "arisen" in the sense of "gone after having been." The *Atthasālinī* and the *Mūlaṭīkā* paraphrase the first part of that compound (*bhūta*) by *anubhavitvā*, "having experienced," and, alternatively, by *bhavitvā*, "having been." In the first case it is explained as follows: "By greed, etc., or their opposites, unwholesome or wholesome kamma experiences the taste of the object (*ārammaṇarasaṁ anubhavati*)." We suggest that the "experience of the taste" refers to the evaluation of the object by greed, non-greed, etc., which, as the *Mūlaṭīkā* stresses, can be performed only by kammic consciousness at the stage of impulsion (*javana*). This evaluation impresses a strong mark upon the entire cognitive process, and, together with that associated mark of evaluation, the image of the first perception is taken up by the subsequent states of consciousness.

This may happen in two ways: (*a*) In order to bring about the result of a complete perception such as we are actually aware of, there is required a sequence of several serial processes (*vīthi*) of sixteen moments each. The later *vīthis*, being repetitions or variations of the first, are naturally influenced by the evaluating act of the first *vīthi*. (*b*) Further, on the occasion of a later encounter with the same or a similar object, the original association of it with a feeling of attraction or aversion will greatly prejudice any later evaluation of it. In such ways a certain portion of past kammic energy (*kammavega*), quite apart from its maturing later into kammic result (*vipāka*), is transmitted to present states of consciousness. To this extent this past evaluating experience (*anubhavitvā*), though "having gone" (*bhavitvā*), has *present* significance. Being active within the present, it may well be regarded as belonging to that qualified conception of the "present" implied by the term *uppanna.*

When *bhūta* is explained as *bhavitvā,* "having been," this second category of "things arisen" refers to everything conditioned (*saṅkhata*) which, after having passed through the three phases of its existence in the present, "has gone." If this last explanation had been given alone, we should be inclined to think that *bhūtāpagat'uppanna* referred merely to the use of the word as a past tense. But against this supposition there is firstly the rather involved term *bhūtāpagata,* which would have been unnecessary to express such a simple matter; secondly and particularly, by the emphasis on the evaluating function of kammic consciousness, the first part of the compound (in the sense of "having experienced") receives a greater stress than the second part expressing the fact of "having gone."

We therefore suggest that this second category of *uppanna* is intended to express the share of past mental states in present ones, particularly that of the active, that is, kammic mental states.

3. *Okāsakat'uppanna,* that is, "arisen" in the sense of "opportunity made." It includes (*a*) that *by which* an opportunity is made and (*b*) that *for which* an opportunity is made.

a. The first is the kamma of the past by which an opportunity is made for the arising of its corresponding kammic result. The *Atthasālinī* says (p. 66): "Though being a thing of the past it excludes any other kammic result and makes an opportunity only for its own result." That is to say, though being past, it still exercises a selective and purposive function. Though not being "real" in the sense of present existence, on account of its being "active" in the above sense it has to be included in that wider conception of "actuality" implied by the term *uppanna.* This past kamma "by which an opportunity is made" is identical with that of the previous division ("gone after having experienced"). The difference is that here the persisting of the past kamma refers to its corresponding kammic result (*vipāka*), while in the previous category the other effects of that past kamma have been considered.

b. That "*for which* an opportunity is made" is the corresponding kammic result of the past kamma. Though being a thing of the future, it nevertheless counts as "arisen" in the sense of having a definite opportunity or chance to arise. It is identical with the "things bound to arise" (*uppādino dhammā*) belonging to the above-mentioned triad in the *Dhammasaṅgaṇī* (*uppanna-tika*). About these "things bound to arise," the *Atthasālinī* says (p. 360) that they are not to be regarded as nonexistent (*natthi nāma na hoti*). This is another proof of the dynamic conception of actuality and time to be found in the canonical Abhidhamma and its earliest commentaries.

In this third category of *okāsakat'uppanna*, the relation is shown between certain things of the past and of the future (leaving out the present), both regarded as "arisen."

4. *Bhūmiladdh'uppanna*, that is, "arisen" in the sense of "having obtained soil," that is, fertile soil for the actual arising. This applies to potential defilements (*kilesa*), which are "potential" in the sense of possessing fertile soil from which they may actually sprout when the other conditions for their arising are given. This soil (*bhūmi*) is provided in all three planes (*bhūmi*) of existence by the individual's own five aggregates (*khandha*) as long as the respective defilements are not yet eliminated by one of the stages of awakening (stream-entry, etc.). The *Visuddhimagga*, in an instructive elaboration of our passage (at p. 687), lays particular stress on the fact that this fertile soil for the arising of defilements consists in the individual's own life process and not in the outer world of tempting objects. Here we have a noteworthy reiteration of the fundamental Buddhist doctrine that human beings are not bound by the external world but only by their own craving. Not only the actuality but also the potentiality of bondage is centered in the individual, that is, in the subjective side of the impersonal life process.

In order not to leave any doubt about the meaning of the word "soil" (*bhūmi*) in this context, we shall elucidate it by the example of the visual perception of a pleasant form. Let us suppose that this perception was not followed immediately by conscious craving or enjoyment because it was superseded at once by a much stronger impression on the mind. Nevertheless this "deferred" defilement of sensual desire (*kāmarāga*) for beautiful forms may spring up at some later moment, for example, when that previous visual perception is remembered. The "soil" for its appearance was provided by the aggregates existing at the time of the previous visual perception: the aggregate of corporeality being represented by the eye, etc., the four mental aggregates by the visual consciousness and by the visual perception, the feeling, volition, etc., connected with it. Until the fetter of sensual desire (*kāmarāga-saṁyojana*) is severed on entering the path of the nonreturner (*anāgāmi-magga*), this defilement underlies the continued process of the individual's five aggregates; it is dormant or latent in their foundation or at their root; it is, as it were, the subsoil to that soil. With all these latter terms we have been paraphrasing the Pāli term *anuseti* (cf. *anusaya*, proclivity, latent tendency, disposition), which is used in this connection in the *Visuddhimagga* thus: *tesu tesu* (*khandhesu*) … *kilesajātaṁ anuseti*, "this species of defilement underlies the respective aggregates of existence."

These potential defilements may be compared to dangerous microbes infesting the body, which, though in a latent state, may become active at any moment when conditions are favorable. It is this soil of the aggregates impregnated with potential defilements that is meant by the Abhidhamma categories of "things favorable to defilements, to cankers, etc." (*saṅkilesikā dhammā* and *sāsavā dhammā*) and kindred terms in the triads and dyads of the *Dhammasaṅgaṇī*.

The fourth category of *uppanna* refers to things that may possibly arise in the future. It differs from those future things of the third category "for which an opportunity is made" insofar as these latter things are related to an actual kamma of the past, while the fourth category relates only to the proclivity of things. The things of the third category are therefore to a much higher degree determined than those in the fourth, because, besides cases that are absolutely determined (see note 69), actually any other kind of kamma-result must eventually arise if not effectively counteracted. They are, therefore, nearer the borderline of factual reality than the mere proclivities of the fourth category. This relation to factual reality was probably the principle underlying the sequence of enumeration of the four categories. Beginning with factual reality, that is, "things presently arisen" (*vattamān'uppanna*), the other three divisions progressively decrease in actuality.

It is important to note that according to the *Visuddhimagga* (p. 689) only the things of the fourth category (*bhūmiladdh'uppanna*), that is, *potential* defilements, can be overcome, or, more correctly, prevented from actually arising.

As a historical sidelight it may be added that the views of the Sarvāstivādins about the coexistence of the *dharmas* in all three time periods are reduced to their proper proportions by the commentarial exposition of *uppanna*. It is shown here which *parts* of the past and the future have or may have active and potential significance for the present and may therefore be regarded as actualities, though not realities. But according to the Theravāda this cannot be said of *all* things past and future, and it hardly seems tenable. It is quite possible that this disquisition on the term *uppanna* was partly intended for use as a refutation of the Sarvāstivāda, which was probably already in existence at the time the *ancient* commentaries were being compiled, the original works on which Buddhaghosa based his own commentaries.

It should be mentioned that the commentarial fourfold division of *uppanna* does not appear in the explanation of the "triad of things arisen" (*uppanna-tika*) but of the phrase *kusalaṁ cittaṁ uppannaṁ hoti* at the beginning of the Consciousness Chapter in the *Dhammasaṅgaṇī*. It is said that in this context the first category of "presently arisen" applies, that is, things presently or actually arisen. In the canonical triad itself, *uppanna* is defined by exactly the same words as *paccuppanna*. But as the defining terms are rather noncommittal we must not conclude that the meaning of "presently arisen" necessarily holds true here as well. Also, the statement in the *Atthasālinī* that the "triad of things arisen" extends over two time periods (i.e., past and future) does not necessitate that limitation for "presently arisen," because the commentarial conception of *uppanna* does not comprise the actual *things* of the past but only their persisting energy, that is, their conditioning influence, still active or latent in the present and the future. It has to be noted further that in the commentarial conception of the term *uppanna*, the "things bound to arise" (*uppādino dhammā*) are only a subdivision belonging to *okāsakat'uppannā*, though not mentioned under that name. In the triad, however, they are not included in the term *uppanna* but form a separate class.

Although, as we see, the *Atthasālinī* does not in any way relate the four categories of *uppanna* to the canonical triad, we feel justified in doing so because both groups of terms are obviously intended to introduce a more elastic and dynamic conception of time. So we suggest that the commentarial four categories may be taken to cover the same field as the *uppannā dhammā* and *uppādino dhammā* of the canonical triad. For any further development of Abhidhamma thought it seems to us important to bring into relation, and if possible into agreement, the terminology of the different periods of the Abhidhamma literature, as far as it is philosophically justified, even if, as in our present case, no complete historical proof can be furnished.

4. Concluding Remarks

The past course of movement, and the direction to which a process moves, doubtlessly belong to the co-determining factors of a present situation. Parts of the past and of the future are, though not real, yet *actual*, in the sense of acting on the present. In the life of the individual as well as in human history this fact is illustrated by the powerful influence of traditions and of ideals, the one being the surviving past, the other the anticipated future. But there is still another unreal factor acting upon the present: the potency or potentiality of a situation, comprising its unmanifested possibilities, its neglected aspects, the deliberately excluded alternatives, the roads open but not pursued. Never can all the aspects and potentialities of a situation manifest themselves simultaneously. Some may well appear in the next moment, others in the near or distant future, either after being remembered and taken up consciously or after undergoing a subliminal maturing process. But the significance of these potentialities is not restricted to the future. They are operative in that very moment. For example, the excluded alternatives will influence the speed, the energy, and the duration of the movement proceeding in the direction decided upon. This influence may be retarding or accelerating, according to circumstances. That is to say, these potentialities are co-determining factors of what we may call the "specific weight" of the given situation; and on this "specific weight" depends the amount of influence that the particular moment of consciousness itself is able to exercise. In this connection, whether or not there was conscious awareness of the various potentialities and alternatives is also a relevant factor. Here enters the Abhidhammic distinction of spontaneous (*asaṅkhārena*) and nonspontaneous (*sasaṅkhārena*, "prompted") actions.[73]

The fact that the potentialities of a situation cannot be excluded from a dynamic conception of actuality was not only recognized in the commentarial period of Pāli literature, as illustrated above in our exposition of the term *uppanna*, but cognizance of it is impressively documented in what is probably the oldest part of the canonical Abhidhamma—the *mātikā*. In the *mātikā*, which is elaborated in the *Dhammasaṅgaṇī* and forms also the basis of the *Yamaka* and the Paṭṭhāna, there are no less than nine terms referring to the potentiality of defilements differently classified. We have already mentioned:

Things favorable to defilements (*saṅkilesikā dhammā*)
Things favorable to cankers (*sāsavā dhammā*)

The remaining terms are:

Things favorable to fetters (*saṁyojaniyā dhammā*)
Things favorable to bonds (*ganthaniyā dhammā*)
Things favorable to floods (*oghaniyā dhammā*)
Things favorable to yokes (*yoganiyā dhammā*)
Things favorable to hindrances (*nīvaraṇiyā dhammā*)
Things favorable to clinging (*upādāniyā dhammā*)

When the *mātikā*, that remarkable systematization of reality, was laid down in the Abhidhamma, it was obviously regarded as indispensable not only to distinguish those things that are, for example, defilements or not, from those that are associated with them, but also to include in a special category those things that are favorable to defilements, that is, that provide a fertile soil for them (*bhūmi*), in the sense explained above.

The *Atthasālinī*, in its exegesis of the *mātikā*, gives the following interesting definitions:

> *Things favorable to clinging* are those which, when becoming objects, are favorable (*hita*) to clinging, owing to their connection with (or affinity to) clinging (*upādāna-sambandhena*). *Things favorable to defilements.* By offering themselves as (lit.: making themselves into) objects for a defilement they are liable to it (lit.: deserve it; *arahanti*); or because they have adapted themselves (*niyutta*) to a defilement they cannot escape being its objects.

According to these instructive explanations, those things providing the fertile soil for defilements are, as it were, attuned to the respective defilements; they engage each other like cogwheels; or their relation is like that of bodily susceptibility and a virus.

Only in the light of a dynamic view of actuality that admits the factor of potentiality, and by a dynamic conception of time that admits partial interpenetration of the three time periods, will the importance and the implications of these Abhidhammic terms be fully understood. In calling attention to these neglected but important terms and by pointing out some of their implications, our intention was to appeal for further textual and philosophical investigations in this field.

Appendix 1
The Authenticity of the Anupada Sutta

Mrs. C. A. F. Rhys Davids, in the preface to her translation of the *Dhammasaṅgaṇī,* throws doubt on the authenticity of the *Anupada Sutta* (*MN* No. 111) as a genuine discourse of the Buddha: "The sutta, as are so many, is an obvious patchwork of editorial compiling, and dates, without reasonable doubt, long after Sāriputta has preceded his Master in leaving this world. We have first a stock formula of praise spoken not once only of Sāriputta. Then, *ex abrupto,* this tradition of his fortnight of systematic introspection. Then, *ex abrupto,* three more formulas of praise. And that is all. The sutta, albeit put into the mouth of the Founder, is in no way a genuine discourse."[74]

So Mrs. Rhys Davids, we do not agree at all. There is certainly no reason why we should doubt that the Master in fact remembered with words of praise his great disciple. On the contrary, it would have been strange if he had not done so. Instead of sharing Mrs. Rhys Davids' impression that the parts of the discourse succeed each other abruptly it seems to us quite natural that, between the words of praise at the beginning and the end, there should be embedded an illustration to this eulogy of Sāriputta's wisdom, namely, the account of his period of analytical introspection, as an example of his penetrating wisdom. The use of set formulas is by no means peculiar to the *Anupada Sutta* but can be met with throughout the Sutta Piṭaka. It can scarcely be maintained that all the numerous texts in which stock passages occur are "compilations" and that these passages themselves are consequently insertions.

Even if the *Anupada Sutta* were a compilation, this would not exclude the possibility that the single parts composing it were the authentic words of the Buddha. "But," Mrs. Rhys Davids says, "the intrusion of two words—of *anupada,* and of *vavatthita,* 'determined'—which are not of the older idiom, suggest a later editing." Though *anupada* does not occur frequently in the Piṭakas, it is also not at all an expression characteristic of any later period of Pāli literature; so we cannot draw any conclusions from the mere fact of its rare occurrence. With regard to the other word, it is true that derivatives of the verb *vavattheti*, *vavatthita*, and particularly *vavatthāna*, are found very frequently in later canonical books such as the *Paṭisambhidāmagga* and the *Vibhaṅga*, and especially in the commentaries and the *Visuddhimagga*. But *vavatthita*, "determined" or "established," is likewise not such a highly technical term that the dating of a text could be based on that evidence alone. There are many other words too which occur only once or sporadically in the Sutta Piṭaka. Even if one of these words, for example *vavattheti*, became the fashion in later idiom in preference to its synonyms, such a development (very frequent in the history of words) does not exclude the occasional use of the same word in an earlier period too.

Mrs. Rhys Davids writes further: "Buddhaghosa either did not know the *Anupada Sutta* or forgot to quote it. Yet to quote it, is precisely what he would have done just here, when he was writing the *Atthasālinī* on the *Dhammasaṅgaṇī*. And his canonical erudition was remarkable. How did he come to overlook the sutta?" He did not overlook it. But Mrs. Rhys Davids has overlooked the fact that Buddhaghosa's commentary to the *Majjhima Nikāya* deals, of course, also with the *Anupada Sutta*. Besides, at *Asl* 208, Buddhaghosa makes a quite unmistakable allusion to that sutta by mentioning the most characteristic term occurring in it, *anupada-dhamma-vipassanā* (see p. 49), an expression that does not, to our knowledge, appear anywhere else in the Piṭakas. It need not surprise us that Buddhaghosa did not quote the incomplete List of Dhammas as given in that sutta. In commenting on the *Dhammasaṅgaṇī*, he was not concerned with historical research, and besides, he did not need to prove what was quite evident at his time: that the Abhidhamma has deep, widespread roots in the suttas. Only today has it become necessary to emphasize the latter fact against such hypercriticism as that of Mrs. Rhys Davids, who goes even so far as to say (p. xii) that the "Abhidhamma… is not the message of the Founder; it is the work of the monkish world that grew up after him." It is to be regretted that such a gifted scholar as Mrs. Rhys Davids marred the value of her later works by hasty and prejudiced judgments.

In conclusion, we repeat that we do not see any reason why the *Anupada Sutta* should not be regarded as an authentic discourse of the Buddha. We therefore feel fully justified in quoting that discourse as a sutta source for Abhidhamma terminology.

Appendix 2

The Omission of Memory from the List of Dhammas

When we were discussing the faculties in the List of Dhammas we noted in passing that *sati* occurs only in "good consciousness" (*sobhana-citta*). This implies that *sati* means here first of all *sammā-sati*, right mindfulness, referring to the four "foundations of mindfulness" (*sati-paṭṭhāna*). The original meaning of *sati* (Skt *smṛti*) as "memory" is, however, not quite excluded, since it has its place in the definition given in the *Dhammasaṅgaṇī*, but it stands rather in the background and refers always to "good consciousness." The question now suggests itself: Why has such an important and frequent mental function as that of memory not been expressly included in the List of Dhammas in its quality as an ethically neutral factor? We cannot suppose that it has simply been forgotten. Against any such explanation stands the fact that this list is too obviously the product of a mind working with the greatest accuracy. The list is undoubtedly the result of careful investigation supported by introspective intuition. Certainly no essential aspects of the subject matter have been overlooked here—though, of course, the list does admit of condensation as well as extensions.

This question of memory as an ethically neutral function was actually raised in the *Atthasālinī*. Here is the passage in full (p. 249):

> In this (unwholesome) consciousness faith, mindfulness, wisdom, and the six qualitative pairs have not been included. And why? There is no faith in an unbelieving mind, therefore that has not been included.... And there is no mindfulness in a mind unguarded by mindfulness, therefore that has not been included. How then, do not adherents of wrong views remember their own deeds? They do. But that is not *sati* ("mindfulness"). It is merely an unwholesome thought process occurring in that aspect (*ten'ākārena akusalacittappavatti*). That is why *sati* is not included (in unwholesome consciousness).

> But why, then, is wrong mindfulness (*micchā-sati*) mentioned in the suttas? For the following reasons: because unwholesome aggregates (*khandha*) are devoid of mindfulness; because it is the opposite of mindfulness; and in order to complete the group of factors of the wrong path (*micchā-magga*). For these reasons wrong mindfulness is mentioned in an exposition of relative validity (*pariyāyena*). But in an exposition of absolute validity (*nippariyāyena*) it has no place.

We cannot say that these explanations are very satisfactory. They still leave unanswered the question why memory has not been included in the list under some other name, such as *paṭissati*, to distinguish it from *sammā-sati*.

In the subcommentary to the passage just quoted from the *Atthasālinī*, we find, however, a hint for a plausible theory about the omission of memory (*DhsMṭ* 120): "[According to that passage just quoted] wrong mindfulness is explained as the unwholesome aggregates that are devoid of mindfulness and contrary to it. This again should be understood as follows: When reflecting on what was done long ago, for example, in the case of inimical feelings, those unwholesome aggregates are associated with keen perception (*paṭusaññā-sampayutta*)."

Taking up this suggestion we can assume that ancient Buddhist psychology ascribed the main share in the process of recollection to perception (*saññā*), regarding it merely as a department of the latter. It should be recalled that *saññā* belongs to the pentad of sense-contact and to the factors common to all consciousness (*sabbacittasādhāraṇa*), so that the requirement of universal occurrence as a neutral and general factor is fulfilled. We are supported in our theory by the definition of *saññā* found in the *Atthasālinī* (p. 110). There two sets of explanations are supplied, given in the customary categories used for definitions (*lakkhaṇa, rasa,* etc.). According to the first explanation, the characteristic (*lakkhaṇa*) of perception, applicable to all cases, is "perceiving" (*sañjānana*, lit. "cognizing well"); the essential property or function (*rasa*) is "re-cognizing" (*paccabhiññāṇa*), said to be applicable only to certain cases, namely, when perception proceeds with the help of a distinctive mark of the object, either fixed to it intentionally (e.g., as by woodcutters to trees) or being a characteristic of the object itself (e.g., a mole in the face of a man). The second explanation is said to apply to all cases of perception. The characteristic is again "perceiving." The essential property given here is: "making marks as a condition for a repeated perception" (i.e., for recognizing or remembering; *punasañjānanapaccayanimittakaraṇa*). So we may sum up: perception (*saññā*) is the taking up,[75] the making, and the remembering of the object's distinctive marks. In this connection it is noteworthy that "mark" or "signal" is also one of the different meanings of the word *saññā* itself.

Not only the "taking up" but also the "making" and the "remembering" of marks may be relevant to all cases of perception if it is understood as follows: What really happens in a simple act of perception is that some features of the object (sometimes only a single striking one) are selected. The mental note made by that perception is closely associated with those selected features; that is, we attach, as it were, a tag to the object, or make a mark on it as woodcutters do on trees. So far every perception is "a making of marks" (*nimittakaraṇa*). In order to understand how "remembering" or "recognizing," too, is implied in every act of perception, we should mention that according to the deeply penetrative analysis of the Abhidhamma the apparently simple act of seeing a rose, for example, is in reality a very complex process composed of different phases, each consisting of numerous smaller combinations of conscious processes (*cittavīthi*), which again are made up of several single moments of consciousness (*cittakkhaṇa*) following each other in a definite sequence of diverse functions.[76] Among these phases there is one that connects the present perception of a rose with a previous one, and there is another that attaches to the present perception the name "rose," remembered from previous experience. Not only in relation to similar experiences in a relatively distant past, but also between those infinitesimally brief single phases and successive processes, the connecting function of rudimentary "memory" must be assumed to operate, because each phase and each lesser successive state has to "remember" the previous one—a process called by the later Ābhidhammikas "grasping the past" (*atīta-gahaṇa*). Finally, the individual contributions of all those different perceptual processes have to be remembered and coordinated in order to form the final and complete perception of a rose.

Not only in such microscopic analysis of sense perception but also in every consecutive thought process, for example in reasoning, the phase of "grasping the past" can be observed, as for instance when the parts of an argument are connected, that is, when conclusions are built on premises. If that "grasp" of the past is too weak to be effective, one says that one has "lost the thread." The way in which one remembers the earlier phases of one's thought process is likewise through selected marks (*nimittakaraṇa*) because it is neither possible nor necessary to consider all the minor aspects of a thought. But if the "selection" is too incomplete and overlooks essential features or consequences of the past thought, then a faulty argument built on wrong premises follows.

In these two ways we can understand how "remembering," that is, connecting with the past, is a function of perception in general. We can now formulate the following definition: *saññā* is cognition as well as recognition, both being by way of selected marks.

We can summarize our findings as follows:

1. Memory, as we usually understand it, is not mentioned as a separate component of a moment of consciousness because it is not a single mental factor but a complex process.

2. The mental factor that is most important for the arising of memory is perception (*saññā* = *sañjānana*), being that kind of elementary cognition (*jānana*) that proceeds by way of taking up, making, and remembering (i.e., identifying) marks.

3. Apart from what, in common usage, is called "remembering," the reminiscent function of perception in general operates also: (*a*) in the imperceptibly brief phases of a complete perceptual process, the sequence of which is based on the connecting function of "grasping the past phases"; (*b*) in any consecutive train of thoughts where this "grasping of the past" is so habitual, and refers to an event so close to the present, that in normal parlance it is not called "memory," though it is not essentially different from it.

Another reason for the omission of memory from either the components or the classes of consciousness is this: remembrance means merely the fact that a state of consciousness has objects of the past (*atītārammaṇa*). But as mentioned already (pp. 34-35), in the *Dhammasaṅgaṇī* the objective side of the perceptual process is used for the classification of consciousness only in a single instance and refers only to the division into visual objects, etc. The time relation of objects, in particular, does not enter into the classification or analysis of consciousness at all, being irrelevant for that purpose. Still less could the time relation—for example, that of memory—be counted as a separate component of consciousness. In the *Dhammasaṅgaṇī* the time relation of objects is treated separately in the "triad of things with past objects, etc." (*atītārammaṇa-tika*). But the fact that a moment of consciousness has objects of the past does not warrant the inclusion of a separate factor called memory.

As a point of comparison between the Pāli Abhidhamma of the Theravādins and the Abhidhamma of later Buddhist schools, it deserves mentioning that in the lists of *dhammas* compiled by the Hīnayānist Sarvāstivādins and by the Mahāyānist Vijñānavādins, *sati* (= *smṛti*) is given as a neutral factor. It is included there in a group called *mahābhūmikā*, composed of factors common to all consciousness, corresponding to the category of *sabbacittasādhāraṇa* in the Theravāda. The fact that *smṛti* is really intended there as an ethically neutral and not a wholesome factor is also proved by the definition given, in this same connection, in the commentary to the *Abhidharmakośa*: *anubhūtasya asampramoṣa* ("the not forgetting of what has been experienced"). This divergence from the list given in the *Dhammasaṅgaṇī* shows that these old thinkers too had noticed the absence of memory in that list, assuming perhaps that it had been forgotten. But for the reasons given above we think that this omission was not only deliberate but fully justified. In other cases of divergence, too, we have found that, on close examination, the Theravāda's List of Dhammas is far preferable, being based on a much more mature judgment of psychological facts. But here we are not concerned with any such comparative study of Abhidhamma systems.

Notes

Works frequently cited have been identified by the following abbreviations:

A	*Aṅguttara Nikāya*
Abhi-s	*Abhidhammattha-saṅgaha* (in *CMA*)
Asl	*Atthasālinī* (Comy to *Dhs*)
BPS	Buddhist Publication Society
CMA	*Comprehensive Manual of Abhidhamma*
Comy	Commentary
Dhs	*Dhammasaṅgaṇī*
DhsMṭ	*Dhammasaṅgaṇī Mūlaṭīkā* (Burmese-script Chaṭṭhasaṅgāyana ed.)
DN	*Dīgha Nikāya*
MA	*Majjhima Aṭṭhakathā* (Comy to *MN*)
MN	*Majjhima Nikāya*
Mil	*Milindapañha*
Netti	*Nettippakaraṇa*
Paṭis	*Paṭisambhidāmagga*
PTS	Pali Text Society
SN	*Saṁyutta Nikāya*
Skt	Sanskrit
Vibh	*Vibhaṅga*
VibhA	*Vibhaṅga Aṭṭhakathā* (Comy to *Vibh* = *Sammoha-vinodanī*)
VibhMṭ	*Vibhaṅga Mūlaṭīkā* (Burmese-script Chaṭṭhasaṅgāyana ed.)
Vism	*Visuddhimagga*

1. Erich Frauwallner, *Studies in Abhidharma Literature and the Origins of Buddhist Philosophical Systems* (Albany, N.Y.: State University of New York Press, 1995). For the sake of simplicity, throughout this introduction I use the Pāli form "Abhidhamma" except when referring to the titles of works that include the Sanskrit form "Abhidharma."
2. On the three Abhidhamma systems, see Frauwallner, *Studies in Abhidharma Literature,* chap. 2–4, and Kogen Mizuno, "Abhidharma Literature," in *Encyclopaedia of Buddhism* (Government of Ceylon, 1961), Fascicule A–Aca, pp. 64–80.
3. *Asl* 13–17, 31–32.
4. On the use of the word *abhidhamma* in the Sutta Piṭaka, see Fumimaro Watanabe, *Philosophy and Its Development in the Nikāyas and Abhidhamma* (Delhi: Motilal Banarsidass, 1983), pp. 25–36.

5. On the role of the *mātikās* in the genesis of the Abhidhamma, see Frauwallner, *Studies in Abhidharma Literature,* pp. 3–11; Watanabe, *Philosophy and Its Development,* pp. 36–67; and A. K. Warder, introduction to *Mohavicchedanī* (London: PTS, 1961), pp. ix–xxvii. See too Rupert Gethin, "The *Mātikās*: Memorization, Mindfulness, and the List," in Janet Gyatso, ed., *In the Mirror of Memory: Reflections on Mindfulness and Remembrance in Indian and Tibetan Buddhism* (Albany, N.Y.: State University of New York Press, 1992), pp. 156–64.
6. For a detailed account, see Y. Karunadasa, *The Dhamma Theory: Philosophical Cornerstone of the Abhidhamma.* Wheel No. 412/413 (Kandy: BPS, 1996).
7. On the importance of the time factor, in the present book see particularly pp. 28-30, 89-92, 104-114.
8. *Asl* 13, 32, 35.
9. Bertrand Russell, *Our Knowledge of the External World as a Field for Scientific Method in Philosophy* (Chicago: The Open Court Publishing Company, 1914), p. 51.
10. Alfred North Whitehead, *Science and the Modern World* (New York: The Macmillan Company, 1926), pp. 64, 227.
11. *Mil* 87.
12. Āryadeva, *Catuḥśataka,* v. 191.
13. *Asl* 15–17. The text says that he taught the Abhidhamma in the heavenly world especially for the benefit of his mother, Queen Mahāmāyā, who had been reborn as a deity in the Tuṣita heaven.
14. *Guide through the Abhidhamma Piṭaka,* p. 12.
15. The title of the first book of the Abhidhamma, *Dhammasaṅgaṇī,* has been rendered by Ven. Nyanatiloka as "Enumeration of Phenomena."
16. The sense-sphere realm (*kāmadhātu*), the form (or fine-material) realm (*rūpadhātu*), and the formless (or immaterial) realm (*arūpadhātu*). (Ed.)
17. Mrs. Rhys Davids has collected over fifty negative characterizations of Nibbāna in Appendix II to *A Buddhist Manual of Psychological Ethics,* p. 342.
18. See the description of the first type of wholesome consciousness, p. 31.
19. At *Asl* 61 the opposite view is called "the great conceit" or "the great delusion" (*abhimāna*).
20. It is to be regretted that here the statements of *Vibh* are (as is so often the case in the Abhidhamma) rather laconic and only partly elucidated in *VibhA.* It will require patient scrutiny and reflection until at least the most important implications of that text will be clearly understood.
21. (1)–(3) are dealt with in *Vism* chapter 18, (4) in chapter 19, and (5) in chapter 20. (Ed.)
22. *MA* IV 88.
23. Otto Rosenberg, *Die Probleme der buddhistischen Philosophie* (Heidelberg: Harrassowitz, 1924).
24. Sogen Yamakami, *Systems of Buddhistic Thought* (Calcutta: University of

Calcutta Press, 1912), p. 100.

25. See Th. Stcherbatsky, *The Conception of Buddhist Nirvāṇa* (Leningrad: Office of the Academy of Sciences of the USSR, 1927).
26. *Na ca so na ca añño.* See *Mil* 40–41.
27. *Asl* 63–64. The derivation of *citta* (= mind, both Pāli and Skt) from *cittatā* (based on Skt *citra*, "variegated") is, of course, only a play on words for a didactic purpose and is not meant to be taken literally.
28. Sense-contact, feeling, perception, and volition are four of the seven mental factors called, in the later Abhidhamma manuals, *sabbacittasādhāraṇa*, i.e., factors common to all consciousness. See note 40 below.
29. *SN* II 246–47: Cakkhu-viññāṇaṁ... cakkhu-samphasso... cakkhu-samphassajā vedanā... rūpa-saññā... rūpa-sañcetanā.
30. *MN* III 25: Ye ca pathamajjhāne dhammā: vitakko ca vicāro ca pīti ca sukhañ ca cittekaggatā ca; phasso vedanā saññā cetanā cittaṁ chando adhimokkho viriyaṁ sati upekkhā manasikāro—tyāssa dhammā anupada-vavatthitā honti.
31. *Asl* 16, 32, 410.
32. See Appendix 1: The Authenticity of the *Anupada Sutta.*
33. The variant *phassa-pañcaka* is preferable, as *phassa-pañcamaka* means "having sense-contact as the fifth," while *phassa* is always enumerated first.
34. *Netti* 15. The *Nettippakaraṇa* is available in a translation by Bhikkhu Ñāṇamoli, under the title *The Guide* (London: PTS, 1962).
35. The former is at *MA* I 249, the latter at *MA* I 276.
36. E.g., at *Vism* 589 and *Abhi-s* (= *CMA* 77–81). See note 33.
37. The word "jhāna" is used here strictly to represent the meditative absorptions. But since, in the Abhidhamma compounds *jhānaṅga* and *jhāna-paccaya*, "jhāna" is being used in a special sense to signify any state of intense absorption, whether meditative or otherwise, these expressions are rendered "factors of absorption" and "absorption condition" respectively. (Ed.)
38. *VibhA* 23: "A state of consciousness produces corporeal phenomena only when it is not defective in regard to factors" (cittaṁ aṅgato aparihīnaṁ yeva rūpaṁ samuṭṭhāpeti). *VibhMṭ* 18: "*In regard to factors* means in regard to the factors of absorption; for it is the factors of absorption which, together with the consciousness, produce corporeal phenomena" (aṅgato'ti jhānaṅgato; jhānaṅgāni hi cittena saha rūpasamuṭṭāpakāni). Corporeal processes produced by consciousness (*citta-samuṭṭhāna*) include bodily and vocal intimation (*kāya-, vacī-viññatti*), the external expressions of intention.
39. *VibhMṭ* 18.
40. *Sabbacittasādhāraṇa.* The seven are contact, feeling, perception, volition, attention, one-pointedness, and vitality.
41. For details, see *Vism* 384–406.
42. *Asl* 119: Adhimokkhalakkhaṇe indaṭṭhaṁ kāretī ti saddhindriyaṁ.
43. *Vism* 492: Adhipaccasaṅkhātena issariyaṭṭhena.

44. *VibhA* 127: Paṭipakkhābhibhavana.
45. See *Paṭis* II 21–22.
46. *Paṭis* II 209. See too *Vism* 402, 404, 405; *SN* V 282–84.
47. See the title and contents of a book by an eminent practical psychologist, F. Matthias Alexander, *Constructive Conscious Control of the Individual* (London: Methuen, 1923).
48. See *SN* V 158.
49. We shall use the expression "good consciousness" as a rendering of *sobhana-citta*, a later Abhidhamma term coined in order to include not only kammically wholesome (*kusala*) consciousness but also the strong consciousness resulting from wholesome kamma (*kusala-vipāka*) and the functional "good action" of an arahant (*kriya-javana*). See *CMA* 45–46.
50. See *AN* III 375; *Vism* 129–30.
51. See *AN* I 51, whence the name of this group is derived. See too the beautiful exposition of these two qualities at *Asl* 125–27.
52. The commentarial explanation is at *Asl* 130–31, to which I shall often refer. Further clarification is provided at *DhsMṭ* 97.
53. To understand this figurative expression, it may be noted that one of the connotations of *kusala*, "wholesome," given in *Asl* is *ārogya*, i.e., (mental and moral) health.
54. The commentary to this text explains the "luminous mind" as the subconscious life-continuum (*bhavaṅga*), which is "naturally luminous" in that it is never tainted by defilements. The defilements arise only in the active thought process, not in the subliminal flow of consciousness.
55. The two are distinguished in that the one who makes calm the vehicle first attains one of the jhānas (or access concentration) and then develops insight meditation with this as a basis, while the one who makes insight the vehicle does not develop concentration to the level of deep absorption but begins directly with contemplation of the changing processes of body and mind. See *Vism* 587–88. (Ed.)
56. The seven are agitation (present in all unwholesome states), envy, avarice, rigidity, sloth, doubt, and conceit.
57. See *Vism* 462–72; *CMA* 76–90.
58. See Bhikkhu Ñāṇamoli, trans., *The Discourse on Right View: The Sammādiṭṭhi Sutta and Its Commentary.* Wheel No. 377/379 (Kandy: BPS, 1991).
59. They are usually defined by a register of ten terms. In the case of mental one-pointedness in the first wholesome state of consciousness, the definition at *Dhs* §11 runs thus: "Mental stability, composure, steadfastness, nonwandering, nondistractedness, an unwandering mind, calm, the faculty of concentration, the power of concentration, right concentration—this is the one-pointedness of mind present at that time" (yā tasmiṁ samaye cittassa ṭhiti saṇṭhiti avaṭṭhiti avisāhāro avikkhepo avisāhatamānasatā samatho samādhindriyaṁ samādhibalaṁ

sammā-samādhi—ayaṁ tasmiṁ samaye cittass'ekaggatā hoti). (Ed.)

60. The numbers of the types of consciousness correspond to those used by Nyanatiloka Thera in his "Table of the Five Khandhas" in his *Buddhist Dictionary* and *Guide through the Abhidhamma Piṭaka*. The types of consciousness, or *citta*, are defined by their roles in the process of cognition. The following brief, partly oversimplified account of the cognitive process should help to clarify these roles: In the case of a process through one of the physical sense faculties (the eye, etc.), when an object impinges on the sense organ a *citta* arises *adverting* to the object (no. 70). This is followed by the *sense consciousness* (eye-consciousness, etc.), a single *citta* that has the function simply of perceiving the bare sense object (seeing, etc.). The five types of sense consciousness are the results either of wholesome kamma (34–38) or of unwholesome kamma (50–54); hence there are ten *cittas* that can arise in this position. The sense consciousness is immediately followed by a *citta* that *receives* the impression of the object; this citta, again, is the result either of wholesome kamma (39) or of unwholesome kamma (55). Next comes a *citta* that *investigates* the object. This is threefold: when the object is exceptionally pleasant it is a wholesome-resultant associated with joy (40); when the object is pleasant-neutral it is a wholesome-resultant associated with neutral feeling (41); when the object is unpleasant-neutral it is an unwholesome-resultant associated with neutral feeling (42). Next arises a "functional" *citta* (neither kammically active nor kamma-resultant) that *determines* or defines the object (71). This is followed by a series of kammically potent *cittas* called *javana*, in which an originative response is made to the object; the *javana cittas* (of fifty-five types) generate either wholesome or unwholesome kamma, except in the case of the arahant, whose *javana* process is not kammically determinate but functional (*kiriya-javana*). In certain cases the *javanas* are followed by two *cittas* that *register* the object. The function of registration may be performed by *cittas* 40, 41, 56 as well as by others not shown in the present table (certain types of *cittas* being capable of performing more than a single function). In a "mind-door process," i.e., a conceptual or reflective thought process, the first active *citta* to arise is the mind-door adverting *citta* (71, in a role different from determining). This is followed by the *javana* phase, then by registration. The three types of investigating consciousness (40, 41, 56) also function as the "connecting thread" of subliminal consciousness arising at the moment of conception (*paṭisandhi*, "relinking"), persisting as the subliminal life-continuum (*bhavaṅga*), and "signing off" at the end of the life span as the death consciousness (*cuticitta*). No. 72 is a weak type of *javana* consciousness that arises in an arahant when he smiles about sensory phenomena. The doubting consciousness (32) is another type of *javana citta*, a weak type because of its inability to take a firm stand. For details, see *CMA* 40–45, 122–29. (Ed.)

61. Russell, *Our Knowledge of the External World*, p. 117.

62. *Asl* 58: Taṁ taṁ upādāya paññatto kālo vohāramattako.... So pan'esa sabhāvato avijjamānattā paññattimattako evā ti veditabbo.
63. *Asl* 112. This holds good also of the *bhavaṅga*, the life-continuum. The word *aṅga* in the compound *bhavaṅga* is usually explained in the commentaries by *kāraṇa*, "cause"; accordingly the entire term would mean literally "cause (or condition) of (continued) existence." But we would suggest that *aṅga* may here have the alternative meaning of "link" as well, and consequently *bhavaṅga* would signify "link of existence."
64. William James, *The Principles of Psychology* (New York: Henry Holt and Company, 1890), p. 639.
65. Leaving aside the preceding moment during which the object existed without being perceived, which properly does not belong to the process itself.
66. See, e.g., the well-known passage in the *Itivuttaka* (no. 27): "Just as the light of the stars is in its intensity not the sixteenth part of the light of the moon, likewise all those meritorious actions forming the basis (of rebirth) are, in their value, not the sixteenth part of love, the liberation of heart."
67. *VibhA* 25: Rūpaṁ garupariṇāmaṁ dandhanirodhaṁ, arūpaṁ lahupariṇāmaṁ khippanirodhaṁ.
68. This is an allusion to the Abhidhamma conception of the four causes of corporeal phenomena; see *CMA* 246–52.
69. On the positive side, definite determination of the future holds for those who reach the four stages of awakening: the stream-enterer is assured of reaching final liberation after at most seven more births, none below the human level, the once-returner of one more birth in the sensuous realm, the nonreturner of rebirth in the form realm, and the arahant of never again taking any birth. On the negative side, those who commit the "five heinous crimes" (parricide, matricide, etc.) or adopt a morally pernicious wrong view are bound to take rebirth in the realms of misery.
70. Similarly, the sutta continues, "It is" is the appropriate designation for present things, not "It has been" or "It will be"; and "It will be" is the appropriate designation for future things, not "It has been" or "It is."
71. This discussion is based on *Asl* 420 and the parallel passage at *Vism* 431.
72. At *Asl* 66 and the parallel passage at *Vism* 687.
73. See also p. 90, where the importance of the factor of potentiality has been dealt with in another context.
74. *A Buddhist Manual of Psychological Ethics*, pp. vii–ix.
75. *Paṭis* Comy: "Perception means taking up the appearance of a thing" *(ākāragāhikā saññā)*. Note that the Latin word *per-cipere*, from which the English "perceive" is derived, means literally "to seize or take up thoroughly," the prefix *per* corresponding to the Pāli *saṁ* in *sañ-jānana-saññā*.
76. See Aung, *Compendium of Philosophy*, pp. 32 ff.; *CMA* 163–66. The perceptual "phases" distinguished in these works are elaborations by later Abhidhamma scholars and are not found in the older texts.

Bibliography

Aung, Shwe Zan, and C. A. F. Rhys Davids. *Compendium of Philosophy.* London: PTS, 1910, 1979. Translation of *Abhi-s.*

Bodhi, Bhikkhu, ed. *A Comprehensive Manual of Abhidhamma.* Kandy: BPS, 1993. Pāli text, translation, and explanation of *Abhi-s.*

Horner, I. B. *Milinda's Questions.* 2 vols. London: PTS, 1963. Translation of *Mil.*

Ñāṇamoli, Bhikkhu. *The Dispeller of Delusion.* 2 vols. London: PTS, 1987; Oxford: PTS, 1991. Translation of *VibhA.*

———. *The Guide.* London: PTS, 1962. Translation of *Netti.*

———. *The Path of Discrimination.* London: PTS, 1982. Translation of *Paṭis.*

———. *The Path of Purification.* 5th ed. Kandy: BPS, 1991. Translation of *Vism.*

Nyanatiloka Mahāthera. *Buddhist Dictionary.* 4th rev. ed. Kandy: BPS, 1980.

———. *Guide through the Abhidhamma Piṭaka.* Kandy: BPS, 1971.

Rhys Davids, C. A. F. *A Buddhist Manual of Psychological Ethics.* London: Royal Asiatic Society, 1923. Translation of *Dhs.*

Thittila, Ashin. *The Book of Analysis.* London: PTS, 1969. Translation of *Vibh.*

Tin, Maung and C.A.F. Rhys Davids. *The Expositor.* 2 vols. London: PTS, 1921. Translation of *Asl.*

Index

A

Abhidhamma literature:
commentaries, xi-xii, 83, 111, 116
interrogations in (*pañhāvāra*), xiv
manuals, xxiv-xxv
and consciousness, states of, xxii
and *dhamma* theory, xvi-xvii
memorization of, xii-xiii
and Sāriputta, 50
subcommentaries (tikas), xii, 120
terminology of, 5, 115-16
time dimension in, 100
See also specific texts
Abhidhamma philosophy:
descriptive nature of, 21
elaboration of, xiii, xiv-xv, 16, 50, 51
twofold method of, 19-30, 43, 106
vitality of, xxiii, xxvii-xxviii, 17
Abhidhamma Piṭaka:
as Buddha's Word, xiii, 2, 13-15, 50-51, 116
classification in, xvii-xix, 11
criticisms of, xxiii, 13
destruction of, ix, x
evolution of, ix-x, xiii-xv
and master lists (*mātikās*), xiv, 10, 51, 113
origin of, xiv, xv, 50-51
Sāriputta in, 50-51
suttas in, xiv, 116
translations of, vii, x, 1
on memory, 123
purposes of, xviii, xx, 4, 17
terminology of, 5, 12-13, 16
versions of, x, xv
See also Palī Abhidhamma Piṭaka
Abhidhamma Studies (Thera), vii-viii, xxii-xxv
Abhidhammattha-Saṅgaha (Anuruddha), xii-xiii, 37, 83, 88, 91
Abhidharmakośa (Vasubandhu), x, 123
abhivinaya, xiv
absorption, factors of (*jhānaṅga*), 53-57
examination (*vicāra*), 32, 49, 54, 56-57, 61
pleasure (*sukha*), 32, 49, 54, 61-62, 72, 77
rapture (*pīti*), 32, 49, 54, 57, 61-62
thought (*vitakka*), 32, 49, 54, 56-57, 61, 66
and ethical qualities, 57
intensifying, 53-57, 61-62
rational, 54
See also jhāna; mental one-pointedness
abstinance, 34, 66, 70
Ācariya Ānanda, xii
Ācariya Anuruddha, xii, 49
Ācariya Buddhaghosa, xi-xii, 51, 116
Ācariya Dhammapāla, xii
accomplishment, bases of, xvii, xviii
actions, bodily, 34, 66, 70
actuality, xviii, 5, 16, 111, 114
aggregates (*pañcakkhandhā*):

as faculty, 32, 61, 63, 66, 85
intensity of, 85-87
as path factor, 32, 40, 66, 67, 85
as spiritual power, 32, 85
as undistractedness, 82-83
See also mental one-pointedness
conditionality, modes of, 24, 28, 43, 53, 58, 94
conditionality, principle of, 22-23, 96
Confucius, 5
consciousness:
as aggregate, xvii, xviii, 48
as *citta-iddhipāda*, xviii
ethical qualities of, xxi, 33-34
factors common to all, 55, 121, 125
functional, xxi, 85
of infinite space, 104
kammic, 46, 100, 107, 108
consciousness, moment of:
duration of, 100
indivisibility of, 23
and meditation, 6-7
and memory, 121, 122
plurality of relations in, 46
consciousness:
realm of, 3
resultant, xxi, 85, 86, 108
sense, 35
in sense-contact pentad, 32, 49, 52, 58
supramundane, xxi, 72, 85
and time dimension, xxii, xxiv, 40, 90, 93-98, 100, 123
typology of, xx-xxii, 83, 129
unwholesome, 83, 85, 119
wholesome (good), 22, 31, 83, 85, 119
See also mind
continuity, 25, 95
craving, 2, 45, 109, 110

D

Davids, C. A. F. Rhys, Mrs., 115-17
decision (*adhimokkha*), 34, 49, 83, 84
defilements, xvii, xviii
anxiety, 74, 79
conceit (*māna*), 74
dogmatism, 74
as evil factors, 80
four taints (*āsava*), xvii, 79
ill will, 79
indulgence in *jhāna*, 11
potential, 109-11, 113-14
rigidity and sloth, 73, 79
ten fetters (*saṁyojana*), xvii, 65, 110
See also hindrances
delusion, xxi
non-delusion, 33, 35-36, 69
dependent origination, xxiv, 21, 24, 43, 96
desire:
covetousness, 33, 69
as craving, 2, 45, 109, 110
for ego-identity, 45
sensual, xviii, 75, 79, 110
for substantiality, 45
Dhamma:
and Abhidhamma, xxvii-xxviii, 15-17
and classification, xix
explanation of, 5
inner logic of, xiv
Nibbāna as goal of, xv, 15
summary statements of, 51
teachers of, 12-13

See also Buddha, teachings of
dhamma theory, xvi-xviii
dhammas:
analysis of, xviii
classification of, xvii, xviii, xix
See also List of Dhammas
conditional nature of, xvi, 41
explanation of, 40-41
lists of, 83, 84, 123
as ontological factors, xv
as "thing-events," xvi, xvii, xix, 23
See also phenomena
Dhammasaṅgaṇī, x, 19
analytical approach of, x-xi, 26, 91
as Buddha's Word, 8
and classifications, 1, 5, 123
attribute-*mātikā*, xv, xviii-xix, 113
"catalog of things," 3, 105
"Enumeration of Phenomena," 20, 21, 103
triads and dyads, xix, 10, 11-12, 78, 82-83, 110
See also List of Dhammas
commentary on. *See Atthasālinī*
Consciousness Chapter of, ix, xxii, 31, 34, 111
samaya in, 6
strands of thought in, xv-xvi
Summary Section of (*Saṅgahavara*), 38, 47, 53, 55, 88
translation of, vii, xxvii, 115
dharmas, 42-43, 106, 111
Dharmguptaka tradition, x
Dhātukathā, x, xi, xix
differentiation, 46, 60
dread, moral, 32-33, 64, 65-66, 70-71

E

effort, as path factor, xvii, 23, 32, 66
ego, 9, 25, 26
elements, xvii, xviii
in Abhidhamma Piṭaka, x
five cognitive, xxii
in Sutta Piṭaka, 15
energy:
as exertion, 82-83
intensity of, 87
kammic, 100-101, 108
as mental factor, 23, 32, 49, 61, 66, 67
as "quiet strength," 72
relational, 29-30
as spiritual power, 32
as unceasing activity, 67, 72
enlightenment:
aids to, xvii-xviii
of Buddha, xiii, xxiv, 2
and Middle Way, 30
perfect (*sammā sambodhi*), 14
seven factors of, xvii
and tranquillity, 72, 77
equanimity, 49
as mental equipoise, 34, 60
ethical qualities:
indeterminate, xxi-xxii, 57, 86, 104
unwholesome, xxi
qualities excluded from, 119-20
roots of, xxi, 57, 75
wholesome, viii-ix, xxii
four planes of, xxi, 53, 56, 72
and fruits of liberation, xxi
roots of, 33, 35-36, 57, 69-70, 73
and supramundane paths, xxi, 65, 69, 82

and "bare attention," xvi-xvii
of Buddha, xiii, 7
helpers for, 34, 82
insight, 9
and Abhidhamma theory, xii, xxiv, 17
investigation of, xii
subjects of, 11-12
introspective, 6-7
misinterpretation in, xxiii, 10-11
and "paired combination," 40, 82
subjects of, 51
and tranquillity, 11
See also cessation
memorization, xiii, xiv
memory (*smṛti*), 119-23
mental formations, xvii, 48, 84
mental one-pointedness (*cittass'ekaggatā*):
as concentration, 54-55, 61, 85
as factor of absorption, 40, 55, 6-57, 62, 72
as mental factor, 32, 49
middle path, 79, 81, 83, 96
Middle Way, 30
Milinda, King, 7, 52
Milindapañha, 7, 52, 84
mind (*citta*):
clarity of, 34, 60, 69, 81
as faculty, xvii, xviii, 32, 62
and kammic energy, 101
and phenomenology, 6
purification of (*bhāvanā*), 80-81
synthesizing by, xvi-xvii
training of, xx, 4, 6-7, 10
velocity of processes in, 100
See also consciousness; qualitative
mental factors
mindfulness (*sati*):
cultivation of, 12, 60
as faculty, 32, 61, 63, 66, 119-20
four foundations of, xvii, xviii, 119
as helper (*upakāraka*), 34, 81
introspective, 6-7
and *jhāna* consciousness, 49
as path factor, xviii, 12, 32, 66, 119
as spiritual power, 32
monastic discipline, xiii, xiv
Mulatika (Ānanda), xii, 41, 54, 73, 82, 107
Myanmar, x, xiii

N

neither-perception-nor-nonperception, 102-03
Nettippakaraṇa, 51-52, 84
Nibbāna:
attainment of, xv, xxi, 15
as *dhamma*, xvi, 20
and liberation, xx, xxi
nature of, xvi, xviii, 20, 104
Nietzsche, Friedrich, 3
Noble Eightfold Path, xviii, 56, 68
See also path factors
non-covetous action (*anabhijjhā*), 33, 69
non-delusion (*amoha*), 33, 35-36, 69
non-greed (*alobha*), 33, 35, 69
non-hatred (*adosa*), 33, 35, 69, 73
non-ill-will (*avyāpāda*), 33, 69
Nyanaponika Thera, vii-viii, x, xv, xxii-xxiv
Nyanatiloka Mahāthera, vii, xxv, 15, 19

O

ontology:
and *dhamma* theory, xvi
versus phenomenology, xvi, 19

P

Paccayākāravibhaṅga, 24
Palī, India, x, 1
Palī Abhidhamma Piṭaka (Theravāda version):
and memory, 123
seven treatises of, x-xi
and attribute-*mātikā*, xix
commentaries on, xi
See also specific treatises
survival of, xiii
and ultimate actualities, xviii
Palī Canon, xv, 19
Palī language, xi, 31
Pañcappakaraṇa-aṭṭhakathā
(Buddhaghosa), xi
Pāṭaliputta, Mauryan empire, xv
path factors (*maggaṅga*), 23, 66-69
liberating function of, 67, 70, 89, 90
listed, 32, 66
and value-attribution, 67, 70
and The Way, 68-69
Paṭisambhidāmagga, 59, 116
Paṭṭhāna ("Book of Origination"), 19
as Buddha's Word, 8
commentary on, xi
and conditional relations, xix, 3, 22, 24, 26, 28, 53, 90
and master lists (*mātikās*), 113
synthetic approach of, x-xi, xxiii, 26, 92
tabular arrangement of, 1
Pēlēne Vajirañāna Mahāthera, 16
perception, xxii
as aggregate, xvii, 32, 48
and analysis of objects, 29, 35
duration of, 100
and memory, 120-23
neither-perception-nor-nonperception, 102-03
in sense-contact pentad, xvii, 32, 48, 49, 52, 120
personality, 3, 62, 97
phenomena:
classification of, xi, xvii, 20
conditional nature of, xi, xxiii, 28, 90
corporeal, 20, 53-54, 57, 58, 59, 61
dependent origination of, xxiv, 21
egolessness of, 26
exclusions from, 104
incorporeal, 83
material, xviii, xxii, 100-101
See also dhammas; experience
phenomenology:
and mind, 6
versus ontology, xvi, 19
Platonic theory, 40, 43
pleasure, xviii, 32, 49, 54, 61-62, 72, 77
potentialities, 55, 90, 112-13
power:
four roads to (*iddhipada*), 59
psychic (*iddhividha*), 57, 59
supernormal, 78
powers (*bala*), 32, 63-66
five spiritual, xvii, 62, 69, 85
listed, 32
stability of, 64-65
Puggalapaññatti, x, xi

Q

R

S

T

About the Author

Ven. Nyanaponika Thera was one of the foremost interpreters of Theravāda Buddhism in modern times. Born into a working class Jewish family in Hanau, Germany, in 1901, with the name Siegmund Feniger, he became a Buddhist by self-conviction before his twentieth year. In 1936 he left Germany for Sri Lanka, where he entered the Buddhist monastic order as a pupil of Ven. Nyanatiloka Mahāthera, the first Theravāda Buddhist monk from Germany. Ven. Nyanaponika participated in the Sixth Buddhist Council in Yangon (1954–56) and was a cofounder of the Buddhist Publication Society in Kandy, which he served as its longtime president and editor. At the time of his death in 1994 he was one of the four "Living Ornaments of the Teaching" in the Amarapura Nikāya, the monastic fraternity into which he had been ordained. His other publications in English include *The Heart of Buddhist Meditation* and *The Vision of Dhamma.*

About the Editor

Bhikkhu Bodhi is an American Buddhist monk from New York City who was ordained in Sri Lanka in 1972. He is currently the president and editor of the Buddhist Publication Society. His books include *The All-Embracing Net of Views, A Comprehensive Manual of Abhidhamma,* and (as a co-translator) *The Middle Length Discourses of the Buddha.*

The Buddhist Publication Society

The BPS is an approved charity dedicated to making known the Teaching of the Buddha, which has a vital message for people of all creeds. Founded in 1958, the BPS publishes a wide variety of books and booklets covering a great range of topics. Its publications include accurate annotated translations of the Buddha's discourses and standard reference works, as well as original contemporary expositions of Buddhist thought and practice. These works present Buddhism as a dynamic force that has influenced receptive minds for the past 2500 years and is still as relevant today as it was when it first arose. A full catalog of our publications will be sent upon request. Write to:

The Hony. Secretary
Buddhist Publication Society
P.O. Box 61
54, Sangharaja Mawatha
Kandy • Sri Lanka
Tel & Fax: 94 08 223679
E-mail: bps@mail.lanka.net
Visit our website at: http://lanka.com/dhamma

About Wisdom Publications

Wisdom Publications, a not-for-profit publisher, is dedicated to making available authentic Buddhist works for the benefit of all. We publish translations of the sutras and tantras, commentaries and teachings of past and contemporary Buddhist masters, and original works by the world's leading Buddhist scholars. We publish our titles with the appreciation of Buddhism as a living philosophy and with the special commitment to preserve and transmit important works from all the major Buddhist traditions.

If you would like more information or a copy of our mail-order catalogue, please contact us at:

Wisdom Publications
199 Elm Street
Somerville, Massachusetts 02144 USA
Telephone: (617) 776-7416
Fax: (617) 776-7841
E-mail: info@wisdompubs.org
Web Site: http://www.wisdompubs.org

The Wisdom Trust

As a not-for-profit publisher, Wisdom Publications is dedicated to the publication of fine Dharma books for the benefit of all sentient beings and dependent upon the kindness and generosity of sponsors in order to do so. If you would like to make a donation to Wisdom, please contact our Somerville office.

Thank you.

Wisdom Publications is a non-profit, charitable 501(c)(3) organization and a part of the Foundation for the Preservation of the Mahayana Tradition (FPMT).